letters to a
young gymnast

Nadia Comaneci

letters to a
young gymnast

BASIC
BOOKS

A Member of the Perseus Books Group
New York

Published by Basic Books
A Member of the Perseus Books Group

The text includes excerpts form *Feel No Fear: The Power, Passion, and
Politics of a Life in Gymnastics*, by Bela Karolyi and Nancy Anne
Richardson. New York: Hyperion, 1994.

Books published by Basic Books are available at special discounts for
bulk purchases in the United States by corporations, institutions, and
other organizations. For more information, please contact the Special Markets Department at the Perseus Books Group, 11 Cambridge
Center, Cambridge, MA 02142, or call (617) 252–5298, (800)
255–1514 or e-mail specialmarkets@perseusbooks.com.

Library of Congress Cataloging-in-Publication Data
Comaneci, Nadia, 1961-
    Letters to a young gymnast / Nadia Comaneci.
        p. cm.
    ISBN 0-465-01276-0
    1. Comaneci, Nadia, 1961-. 2. Gymnasts--Romania--Biography.
3. Gymnastics. I. Title.
GV460.2.C65A3 2003
796.42'092--dc22

                                                    2003017268

04 05 06 / 10 9 8 7 6 5 4 3 2 1

This book is dedicated to my best friend and husband Bart Conner. We have come a long way since our first kiss in 1976 and I cannot imagine anyone else to make this journey with or whom I am more proud to call my partner.

I want to thank my family for all of their love and support and Paul Ziert for his kindness and friendship.

To the people of Romania I say that I am proud to be one of you and to call our country my home.

My thanks also to Nancy Richardson Fischer for the talent, enthusiasm, and energy she brought to the writing of this book.

—Nadia

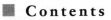 Contents

Introduction   *ix*

The Dream   1
The Beginning   15
Necessity   23
The Disciplined Life   47
Tough Teens   59
The Scorpion   71
Courage?   93
The Struggle   107
The Scream   115
Fairy Tales   131
Defection   137
Doing Time   151
A Breath of Fresh Air   167

About the Author   179

Dear Nadia,
    Tell me everything . . .

Dear Friend,
    I don't know everything. You have asked me to begin
a correspondence in the hope of learning about my life. I
am reticent. I've never written about myself before because there is not enough time in the world to spend it
looking back.
    You believe that there are answers in my past to the
questions of dedication, strength, courage, pressure,
goals, dreams, triumphs, challenges, and love. I look at
those words and they slide from the page into chapters
that I rarely visit. But you tempt me to recall forgotten
stories and relive moments of happiness and hell.
    I will try to answer your letters with the hope that my
experiences may help you in some small way. Remember
that they are mine and you must build your own story
with both care and wild abandon.

                                        Nadia Comaneci

■ The Dream

There are two gymnastic moves on the uneven bars named after me. The first is called the "Comaneci Salto." *Salto* is a general term for a somersault. To perform a Comaneci Salto, the gymnast begins in a support position on the high bar. She casts away from the bar and performs a straddled front somersault and regrasps the same bar.

Gymnastics skills are rated from the easiest move to the most difficult. An A move is the easiest, then there are B, C, D, E, and Super E moves. The Super E is the most difficult, and usually, only a few gymnasts in the world can perform one. The Comaneci Salto is rated an E move. Even now, many years after the 1976 Olympics, very few gymnasts attempt the Comaneci Salto because it is so difficult.

I have a recurring dream. In it, there are two young girls with long brown hair floating over my bed. They wear gauzy, white nightgowns that fall loosely around pale legs and delicately pointed bare feet. I lie on my back beneath the covers watching them hover. They are lovely creatures, and I am not afraid; I am mesmerized, and I long to join them because they are cloaked by soft light, graceful and pure. Their lips, pale rosebuds, curve into smiles; their brown eyes are wise; their delicate fingers cup together, holding a hidden promise.

And then the dream changes. The girls hover closer, and their mouths open into cavernous, yawning black holes. Suddenly, all I can see is darkness. All I can hear is the roar of a vast ocean. I am cold; I am afraid; I am alone. I know that the blackness will swallow me whole, but my bones are leaden and I cannot move from my bed. I try to call out for help, but the scream catches in my throat. The terror tastes like salt and blood.

And then the dream shifts. I see tiny bursts of color flutter out of the darkness. The girls drift overhead; I am still shrouded by the void, but sapphire, ruby, and amber-colored butterflies with transparent wings dart at the edge of vision . . . first one, then two, then many more. They look like stained glass—delicate, fragile, and breathtaking. The black begins to recede.

I peer into the girls' cupped hands. They are empty, and yet, they hold everything . . . promises, opportunities, desperation, love, angry words, delight, Romania, deception, rag dolls, fairy dust, clarity, applause, my grandmother's smile, tears, fear, red ribbons, barbed wire, practices, curses, surprises, my mother's touch, elation, America, music, the scent of vanilla, refusal, a first kiss, dances, whispers, apple trees, my brother's laugh, the scrape of chalk against my palms, airplanes, sunsets, disappointment, skin and wind and waves, rivals, survival, upheaval, broken words, magic, the feel of my father's hugs, chocolate, passports, fishing trips, funerals, birthdays, proposals.

Sometimes in my dream, fear paralyzes me, and I cannot reach for the girls' hands. The darkness grows again, and I am swallowed and wake gasping for air, my hair drenched with sweat, my heart skipping and racing and grasping. I feel lost then and lonely in my failure. I feel like a child, a teenager, a young woman who never had the opportunity to control her destiny and learned nothing from the years of frustration, confusion, and desolation. I see the ghostlike girls fade from my vision and their almond-shaped eyes fill with regret.

Sometimes, though, I take the girls' hands and gently open them; I let life slide through their fingers because there are moments when I have the courage to risk letting go of everything even though I understand the danger of doing so. Then my bedroom fills with butterflies and bursts of electric color, and the darkness recedes. I am wrapped in the knowledge that I cannot always choose dreams but that I can be lost and found, afraid yet brave, and make each moment my own.

Dear friend, in your letter you asked about my dreams, childhood, and early life as a gymnast. Perhaps you expected short and simple answers. Maybe you wanted to hear about my first perfect score of 10, gold medals, defection . . . I promise all that will come. But my life, like your own, is much more complex than a simple list of failures and accomplishments, and I will not cheat you of your answers despite some discomfort on my part in the telling.

I have come to realize that these letters are not only for you. There is a catharsis that comes from recalling the memories I had carefully packed away in the attic of my mind so that I could go on with my life unburdened by the remembering. You have asked me to shine a light into that dusty place, and I am finally ready to do so. Bear with me. Write me again, and take my hand when I falter because I cannot make this journey alone. I do not know you, but you will know me.

Do you know what they say about stories? That there are always three versions—yours, mine, and the truth. This is mine, and I hope that what I have seen and understood and what I choose to share during our correspondence is valuable for you. Everyone has a few secrets. I will tell you some of mine, but I will keep a few as well because they are either personal treasures or too painful to recall and because I worry about distressing the living or the relatives of the dead with tales that cannot be altered to protect friends and families.

You ask who I am. I was born in Romania on November 12, 1961, and named Nadia Elena Comaneci by my father, Gheorghe, and mother, Stefania. My name literally means "hope," but my grandparents always believed it should have meant "luck." When I made my loud entrance into the world, I had a rare and large birth defect—a sac of liquid on the top of my head that looked like an enormous blister. The Romanian doctors were stymied and told my mother that they weren't certain I would survive and that if I did, I'd have mental handicaps. The doctors stuck me with countless needles, but the problem remained.

Finally, my grandmother instructed my mother to take me to church on Sunday; before the priest entered, she was to carry me over the threshold three times. She did, and when she woke the next morning and took me from my cradle, the birth defect had disappeared. It was probably a coincidence, but that's *her* story and the first lucky thing that happened in my life.

The second lucky incident occurred a week after I left the hospital. My mother was staying at my grandparents' home so that they could help her take care of me. There was a big storm the first night, and the roof was covered with giant slabs of ice. The next day, while I slept in a tiny bed in the kitchen because it was warmest in there, my parents and grandparents repaired windows and leaks. Passing through the kitchen, my grandfather decided to pick me up. A second later, the roof collapsed onto the bed. I would have died if he hadn't been holding me at that moment. It was probably another coincidence, but I grew up Romanian and in the Orthodox Church—and we have a tradition of weaving stories into gifts from God.

My mother once told me that the first piece of meat I ever ate was part of a bird. She believes that is why I loved to be outside, climb trees, and jump from heights without getting hurt and why I was able to soar as a gymnast. She also believes that's why I did not break my neck or drown when I fell off a 5-meter-high bridge as a toddler. By that point, my brother, Adrian, had been born, and he was seated in a stroller while I walked by my mother's side over the bridge. Somehow, my foot got stuck in the wooden slats, and I flipped and fell over the edge and into thigh-deep water.

My mother panicked. She couldn't leave my brother on the top of the bridge and jump after me. First, my brother might have crawled out of the stroller and fallen, too. Second, my mother probably would have killed herself landing in the water, and that wouldn't have done either of us any good. So she raced over the bridge, and by the time she'd reached land, I was already out of the water and waiting for her. All I had were a few bruises. I did not cry. I rarely do.

Everything I feel remains inside, with rare exceptions. I internalize it all, but that's my personality—I don't like to play theater. My face is an impenetrable wall to the outside world. I am like a pond and can be a mirror for your emotions, dear friend, but I rarely allow my own to surface and form ripples on the water. Beneath my calm facade, there are sometimes storms, but I experience them alone and share what I've seen and learned later, in my own way.

As a child, I used to clench my teeth when I felt upset, angry, or frustrated, but I refused to give people the satisfaction of seeing me cry. I've heard my old coach, Bela Karolyi, say that I was the only young gymnast he could never break. Perhaps it has always been an ego thing with me. But it is not an act I put on like a piece of clothing; it is quite simply the way I am.

I have always been a quick learner. At a young age, I figured out that the best way to get what I wanted wasn't by crying. I paid a lot of attention to my parents when they talked and especially when they whispered. If I wanted to go to the zoo, I'd listen to exactly what they thought I needed to do to deserve that treat, and then I'd do it. Manipulative? Yes—but far less annoying to everyone than throwing a fit and bursting into tears. I did the same as a gymnast and channeled frustration or anger into my performance instead of wasting it on less productive feelings. Friend, no one ever accomplishes your dreams for you, regardless of tears, fits, or any other means of manipulation. They can give you ideas and direction, but in the end, you have to do it alone. You must figure out your own destination and the best route to get there because no one else knows the way.

When I was young, life was generally so simple and fun that it was hard to be upset and difficult to find a reason to cry. I spent my days playing outside and visiting my grandmother's farm, where I could dig carrots out of the ground and eat ripe, red tomatoes off the vine, the juice trickling down my chin. There were fruit trees laden with purple, red, yellow, and orange delights, their thick branches stretching toward the sky in thanks. I'd climb as high as possible and then drop, swinging down from branch to branch. There was so much freedom in the feeling of my body slicing through the air, my feet almost touching the clouds, the rough bark beneath my palms, and the scent of fresh grass when I landed in the backyard of my grandmother's house. No wonder that when I was introduced to gymnastics, I took to it like a duck to water—it gave me endless opportunities to soar through the air in ways I'd never before imagined.

I recall that I loved to play soccer, and I used to practice every day so that the boys would allow me to play on their teams. If I wasn't playing soccer or climbing trees, then I was doing cartwheels. The freedom of movement was intoxicating, and I could never stand still. My father was always filled with a sense of joy in life, and I believe I inherited that from him in the joy I get from movement, just as I know that I inherited my mother's intense, cat-like brown eyes.

Fishing—that's another thing I loved to do. My grandmother on my father's side lived beside a little river where the water played soft melodies as it flowed over timeworn rocks. Grandmother and I would take a small, hollow ball and put tiny pieces of cornmeal inside it. Knee-deep in cool water, we'd wait for the fish to dive for the bait, and then we'd cover the hole with our hands and pull our dinner out of the river. We'd fry the tiny fish and eat them whole. I've never tasted anything sweeter than what I've caught with my own hands.

As I said, life was simple back then. My mother smelled like the kitchen because she was always cooking. She was a very energetic woman and did five things at one time very well. My father smelled of oil; he was an auto mechanic who walked 12 miles a day to and from work. He never owned his own car and had no desire to—cars, he used to say, always break down. We lived in the small village of Onesti, cradled in the foothills of the Carpathian Mountains of Romania. There were forests, a few streets, a handful of stores, and tiny European-style homes that made Onesti appear more like a hamlet than a town.

Do you know anything about my homeland? You cannot truly understand a person unless you know where they have come from. I am who my people are and were; what they have gained and lost; the product of their wars, humiliations, revolutions, upheavals, and triumphs. If you want to know me, know Romanians because my spirit was created by their experiences, passed down and given as an offering to our collective future.

Ukraine, the Black Sea, Bulgaria, Yugoslavia, Moldova, and Hungary all border Romania. Moldavia and Transylvania compose the northern half of the country, which is divided down the middle by the Carpathian Mountains. The flat Danube plain of Walachia, with the capital Bucharest, lies south of the east-west line of the Carpathians. In my country, there are sandy beaches, densely forested mountains, and beautiful valleys. There are castles and famous waters known for their miraculous healing powers and places to ride horses and ski. As gymnasts, my teammates and I were taken every year for a relaxation period to some of the most incredible places in Romania—places the average citizen would never have the opportunity to experience. They still exist, despite the ravages that have passed through my country. If you can, try to see them some day.

When I think of Romania, I see the beauty. But its history, like that of all countries, is shaded by killing—for land, people, ideas, and freedom. Romanians are descendants of the Dacian tribe that inhabited the Balkan Peninsula. We were part of the Roman Empire and later were occupied by the Goths. The next to overrun our country were the Huns, then came the Bulgars, Slavs, and Russians. The invaders changed, but the violence remained, and in more recent times, Romanians suffered through the German occupation during World War II. In 1947, the Communists took control of our government, and our country was renamed the Romanian People's Republic.

My memory of the history of my country begins in 1967 when I was six years old and Nicolae Ceausescu was named the first secretary of the Romanian Communist Party. Later, Ceausescu became president. My earliest recollection of our government involved knowing that Ceausescu was my country's leader. I would only learn the extent of his crimes against my people later, after the bloody Christmas Revolution of 1989 when the Romanians finally rose up against his cruel and tyrannical rule.

As a child, all I knew were the tall trees, the mountain breezes, and my family. I was five years old when my brother was born, and I loved him from the moment the stork dropped him down our chimney. Originally, I thought that the stork used the front door, but to explain to me why my brother's skin was a shade darker than my own, my parents devised the chimney story, complete with soot. Despite Adrian's arrival, I was still daddy's little girl—wily, stubborn, and at times indulged. I am not proud of some of the things I did, but I must admit certain of those episodes do reflect my personality, so I will share a few stories with you.

I remember desperately wanting a pair of roller skates and my mother saying we didn't have money to buy them. I refused to accept her answer and convinced my father to go with me to the store, just to try the skates on—the old divide-and-conquer scheme. Once the skates were on my feet and I could feel the speed and power as I sped through the store, I couldn't bear to give them back. I raced onto the street wearing them so that my father was forced to purchase them. I have never been able to take no for an answer.

Another time, I was given a bicycle for my birthday. My father had put it together, but he warned me not to take it outside until he'd tightened all the screws. As soon as he left for work, I rode away, losing both pedals and eventually having the bicycle fall apart beneath me into a pile of pieces. My disappointment and the fact that my father made me wait a week before rebuilding the bike was punishment enough.

My father only spanked me one time in my life. I was seven years old. That morning, the sunshine poured through my window, pried my eyes open, and beckoned me outside with a gleaming finger. I was out of the house before I'd swallowed my breakfast, running down the road to find other children who wanted to spend the day losing themselves in the forests, wading through streams, racing in fields, and scrambling up trees. I didn't return home until after dark that night.

Friend, back then we didn't have telephones in our homes, so I couldn't check in with my parents or ask when I had to be home for dinner. It was both a blessing—because I didn't have to interrupt my fun—and a curse—because my parents had trouble keeping track of me. My father was frightened on the night I came home after dark, for he thought I'd been hurt. There had been a rumor that a dead child had recently been discovered in the basement of a home in a neighboring town. When I came into our yard—whistling, little twigs in my wild and long hair, my backside covered with leaves and dirt—my father was waiting for me by the window. He spanked me once with his belt on my behind and then made me kneel for three hours on cracked walnut shells. He wanted me to be as uncomfortable as he was while waiting for me to return home. I never did anything like that again.

I was a true tomboy, with uncontrollable energy that at times pushed my parents to the limits. They'd come into the house and find me pinned to the ground beneath our Christmas tree because I'd tried to climb it to reach the sweets hung on the top boughs. I wasn't crying under the pine needles—I was eating the handfuls of candy I'd swiped before the tree fell. They couldn't keep sap off my fingers or my clothes pressed and clean, and it was a rare day that I'd stay inside and do what most little girls did, such as play with dolls or help my mother around the house. I was a wild, strange scrap of a girl who was as happy playing alone as I was with friends. I didn't seem to need anyone—at times to my parents' chagrin.

I remember that period of my life as very happy. Although my family had the necessities—food, clothing, and shelter—there were not a lot of extras. There was no gourmet anything and no name brands. Jeans, shirts, and underwear were just clothing, and everyone wore the same thing. Everyone also went to the government doctors for health care; they injected you with medicine or gave you a pill—no choices, no alternatives. For many people, life was drab and colorless because they focused on what they did not have. But as a child, all you see are the endless possibilities.

You have grown up in the United States, and I wonder about *your* childhood. Do you live in a home with central air-conditioning and unlimited heat? I know that not everyone in America is wealthy or has access to what I would have considered luxuries, but what about you? Do you have many modern conveniences? Do you work by computer? Have you ever washed a plate or glass by hand? Do you take long, hot showers; order clothing from catalogs or off the Internet; eat fast food or dine on takeout from Thai restaurants; and chat on a cordless phone in your bedroom? I do not begrudge you any of these things, and I know that the United States is an incredibly diverse country with great riches and poverty. I just want to understand where you come from so that I can help you comprehend how different my life probably was from yours.

When I was a child, our TV was tiny and black and white and only received three government-approved stations. There was no such thing as satellite television, cable, MTV, or HBO. I didn't even conceive of things like dishwashers, microwaves, washing machines, or computers. Today, you can plug myriad gadgets into the wall, and they'll do everything for you. As a child, I learned by creating and figuring out how to make things work (I can figure ways around any problem). Most people go and buy what they need, and if it doesn't work, they buy again. We didn't have that option. But I wouldn't trade my early years for anything.

Adrian, who was my childhood companion and is still my best friend, was a whiz with electronics and used to make cassette recorders for cars and repair televisions without any training. When we were kids, he created a gadget that would make a light flash in our bedroom when our mother stepped on the first stair to come up and check on us. We were always ready when she opened the door, hiding whatever it was we weren't supposed to be doing. It's a bit frightening to imagine what trouble Adrian would have gotten into if he'd had all the options you do!

I've heard people say that you can't go back; can't revisit your childhood; can't relive memories; can't see, touch, or taste the past. But several years ago, I returned to my hometown. I traveled on a dirt road that I remembered as long and winding and over bridges that had seemed unfathomably high. Everything appeared so small. Perhaps that was because I walk as an adult today, with long steps and authority, not as a child whose world seemed enormous even in the confines of a little village. I wandered down the street to the home where I grew up and stood inside the bedroom where my life once revolved around digging for carrots, catching silver fish, and learning how to soar, and I marveled at how large my world has become.

I live everywhere now—Oklahoma, Los Angeles, Bucharest—and have dual citizenship, Romanian and American. I understand politics and freedom and the price paid for defection from your homeland, family, and friends in return for the unknown. I comprehend opening your hands and letting slide everything you are for the promise of what you might one day be. I've found the courage to face real monsters, not the ones perceived beneath my bed, and to keep dreaming even when the landscapes turned to madness and I believed I'd be swallowed by the dark. And those butterflies in my recurring dreams . . . the ones that are ruby, sapphire, and amber and flutter like perfect living works of art? They're real, if you know where to look for them.

The Beginning

The second gymnastics skill on the uneven bars named after me is the "Comaneci Dismount." To perform the Comaneci Dismount, a gymnast begins in a handstand on the high bar and then pikes her feet onto the bar and does a sole circle swing around the bar. She then releases the bar first with her feet and then with her hands as she performs a half-twist immediately into a back somersault dismount. Today, this is rated as a B move. In 1976, it was the most difficult dismount being performed.

In your letter, you asked if I always knew that I was destined to be a great athlete. I remember noticing when I was in kindergarten, only about four years old, that whenever people thought someone was getting too cocky about their abilities, they would say, "If only you could see the size of your nose." It was said to me many times because I believed I was a super athlete, always, and in the case of gymnastics, I was right. Does that sound cocky? I would not say I was the best at swimming or ice-skating, although I believe I could have been quite good at the latter. But to say this about my gymnastics ability . . . well, it has been proven.

But at the start of my career, nothing was proven and gymnastics was simply a pastime, nothing more. I never set out to be "Nadia—the first gymnast to receive a perfect 10 in competition, with a new power and body-type that would change the face of gymnastics forever." Back then, gymnastics didn't bring fame, sports agents, millions of dollars, or your picture on a Wheaties box. For me, it wasn't about the future; it was about the moment and personal accomplishments and eventually representing my country and making my people proud. Romanians have a saying, "Not every dog has a bagel on its tail." It means that not all streets are paved with gold. When I began my career, I just wanted to do cartwheels. It's hard to believe that now, but it's true, my friend.

I was in kindergarten when I joined my first gymnastics team, the Flame. My mother took me to the large gymnasium where the team practiced because she wanted to find an outlet for my excessive energy. Jumping on beds, spending day and night racing around the village, and punching little boys in the nose when they refused to let me play was no longer working for my mother. When I stepped into the gym, I knew I fit into that world—or that I wanted to. I was overwhelmed by its size, by my own shyness, and by the endless possibilities for play that each mat, vault, parallel bar, and beam held.

In Romania, sports are considered a great way to help children develop into healthy adults. For me, gymnastics was introduced casually—there was no pressure and no fear. Though I didn't realize it at the time, the instructors quietly watched to see which children showed the most talent. I still loved soccer, but gymnastics slowly began to eclipse all other sports in my life. I remember that at the end of each class, my instructor, Mr. Duncan, would ask, "Who thinks they've done well today?" We'd all raise our hands, and if he agreed, he'd give each little gymnast a piece of chocolate. I loved chocolate, so the reward may have had something to do with my returning to the gym every day.

You asked in your letter what "the single question" that changed my life was. At first, I was taken aback by your query. Do *you* have a sole question that you remember so vividly? Does one question have the power to set anyone, let alone a child, onto an unchangeable path? Is existence just a matter of fate? I imagine my life as an intricate, swirling line of dominoes and wonder if the touch of a single fingertip on the first ivory rectangle is enough to set the rest into motion, click-clacking one by one until the end of my days.

I guess the single question for me may be buried in history—not just mine but that of the gymnastic world as a whole. It's a history I find difficult to recall because I was only six years old when it all began for me. I remember a big man with a droopy mustache coming to my school class and asking, "Who can do a cartwheel?" The man had bright eyes, and there was something about him that made me want to raise my hand and impress him with what I could do. But I must turn to that man's own words to explain the moment because my memory of that day is a little hazy:

Creating an experimental gymnastic school in Onesti was a dream [Marta and I] had never dared hope for.

It was also one of the most difficult projects we had ever undertaken. . . . We tested about four thousand children. I went from elementary school to elementary school testing for speed, flexibility, coordination, and balance. I set up mats in each classroom and taught the kids somersaults, headstands and backbends. I also organized races and balancing contests. It was fairly easy to see who had flexibility and coordination, even in the youngest children. By the fourth week of testing, we still hadn't found enough kids for the school. And I wasn't satisfied with the physical quality and the natural talent of the children we had found. I decided to screen for gymnasts one more time.

Recreation period is a great time to watch kids without getting directly involved in their activities, and I spent hour after hour watching kids play . . . the children I observed were active, but they weren't gymnasts. Then one day I saw two little blond-headed girls doing cartwheels in the corner of the schoolyard. I approached and watched them very closely—they had something. Brrrring! The school bell rang and the little ones darted inside.

Where did they disappear to? I went from class to class, but I did not recognize the girls' faces. . . . Who likes gymnastics? I'd ask the kids in each classroom I visited. They didn't even know what the word gymnastics meant. Okay, I tried . . . who can do a cartwheel? The kids would raise their hands and I'd have them do a cartwheel for me. "Very nice," I'd say, but they weren't the ones.

I was ready to give up. It was the end of the day and I had been to every class. I stopped for one last try. "Can anyone do a cartwheel?" I tiredly asked. No answer. I was ready to walk out when I saw two little blonde heads in the back of the room. "Hey, can either of you do a cartwheel?" They whispered to each other and then nodded yes. "Let me see them," I said. Boom, boom—they did perfect cartwheels.

"You guys are the ones doing cartwheels in the corner of the schoolyard," I said. They nodded. "What are your names?" I asked them. "Viorica Dumitriu" and "Nadia Comaneci," they answered. I told them to tell their mothers that Bela Karolyi said they could be admitted to Onesti's experimental gymnastics school if they wished.

—Bela Karolyi, from his autobiography, *Feel No Fear*

If I wished?! Gymnastics meant freedom to do the things I couldn't do at home. The experimental school in Onesti, the hostel for boarders, and the gym were all connected in one complex. In the early years, I lived at home and only walked half a mile to the school. Our schedule went six days a week—four hours each day taking classes and four in the gym. I enjoyed math and chemistry, but I craved the moment we were set free and I could race to the gymnasium. It was as if a fence had been unlocked, a chain released, a bolt turned, and the world instantly stood waiting and wide open.

When I received my first leotard, I slept with it on my pillow. It was too big and didn't fit me. The night I took it home, I wouldn't let my mother sleep until she'd sewn a red *N* on the name tag and made me gymnastics shoes and socks (they were not available in the stores, and even if they had been, we couldn't have afforded them). My grandmother had made me a doll out of T-shirt material; it was named Petruta, and I used to sleep with it every night. The doll was immediately replaced with the leotard. Like any child, I had a short-term memory and no loyalty for once loved but readily discarded toys. Everything was forgotten in lieu of gymnastics.

Bela Karolyi and his wife and coinstructor, Marta, put me in a group of young gymnasts. We spent a few hours a day working with weights and ropes and did lots of jumping, running, and other training. They made each day fun, and I had no fear and never said "I cannot do that." Bela tells me now that this trait caught his attention early on, but back then, I was not the star of the little girls' team, Viorica was. I was quiet, never smiled, and rarely stood out from the other gymnasts. We were also surrounded by older girls with much more developed skills, so I always knew I was not the best at the school. But inside, I was bursting to learn new skills and prove myself. It's hard to describe, but I could actually taste how much I wanted to be a better gymnast. I was consumed. Friend, is there anything in life you've desired that much?

I always wanted to do more than Bela or Marta asked of me—if they said twenty-five push-ups, I'd do fifty. I liked the feeling of improving; I craved accomplishments. It took months to learn the simplest skills; a cartwheel on the beam began as one on a mat, then on a line painted on the floor, then on a low beam surrounded by cushions, and finally moved to the high beam. Every day, I'd return to the gym and start all over again until I mastered each skill. I didn't mind because each step, repetition, loss, or gain made me better.

That's life, isn't it? You see what you want, and you strive to become more every day until you can grasp the dream in your hands. It's hard work, but if you do what you love, it's joyful. I was not born a champion, and I did not dream in those early days of becoming one. I dreamed of the little competitions Bela held in the gym and the silly trophies he passed out when we'd done well. I dreamed of learning new skills. I never saw the bigger picture or international success and fame. I dreamed of running and twisting and double somersaults and that nothing could tether me to the ground because I was born to fly.

Have you heard people say that the eyes are the windows to the soul? I have been told that my eyes make people uncomfortable, that they are too intense, too calculating. Some say my eyes do not match my smile and that there is a coldness in them that adults find uncomfortable but to which children are oblivious. I can say only that if my eyes are windows, then I can choose to draw the shades at times. The glimpses I allow into my soul are the product of a conscious decision on my part. I look back on pictures of myself as a young gymnast and understand that some see blankness. But I see intensity, determination, desire. Always desire.

Necessity

I always wanted to do the impossible, so when Bela came up with the idea for the Comaneci Salto, I was eager to try to perfect the skill. A similar move was already being performed from the low bar to the high bar. Bela thought I could do it all on the high bar by catching the same bar I'd released. I spent countless hours, days, weeks, and months perfecting the never before attempted skill.

The reason the Comaneci Salto is so difficult is that there's no room for error. With most elements in a routine, a gymnast can be a little bit off and still successfully complete a skill. With the Comaneci Salto, if you're off even the tiniest bit, you cannot make the element, and you crash big-time. The key to making the Comaneci Salto is to always be the perfect distance from the bar so that you can complete a rotation without hitting it with your heels or missing it with your hands. I used to tape foam to my heels because they got so bruised from constantly whacking the bar. As a result of my determination, the Comaneci Salto was the first big release move seen at the 1976 Olympics.

Friend, do not believe that luck covered me like silk from the moment I was born or that everything I did came easily, without cost. I had a very long road to travel before I achieved any of my goals.

My first big gymnastics competition was the 1970 National Championships—I was nine. I remember Marta, who was my beam coach, telling me minutes before the competition began to show the world what she'd taught me. Concentrate and don't let me down, she instructed. Looking back, I realize that the Karolyis were under enormous pressure to justify their work at the Onesti gymnastics school, which was funded by the Romanian government and originally designed and created by a family named Simionescu. It's hard to express in words my thanks to the Simionescus for bringing to life such an incredible program, to which I owe much of my success. Back then, though, I felt that I, not the Karolyis, had something to prove and that the weight of the world was on my shoulders.

I read a book by Ayn Rand when I was in my thirties, and in it, a character is asked what he would do if he were Atlas and had the weight of the world on his shoulders. He answers, "Shrug." At nine, I was unable to do so. I had practiced countless hours and knew my routine to perfection. But I found myself unable to concentrate because of the pressure I'd put on myself.

I could taste how much I wanted to do well, but with my first high leap, I fell off the left side of the beam. Embarrassed, I climbed back on and immediately fell off the right side. Determined not to fall again, I remounted. My ears burned with the imagined laughter of my teammates and other competitors, and I couldn't bear to think of facing Marta when I was done. I will not fall again, I promised myself. I fell again. I felt shame and stupidity. You fall once, it's a mistake, but twice is a lack of brains. Kids do things wrong, but that was a little much, like hitting myself in the head three times. It was my first taste of failure, and I didn't like it at all. Maybe that is what makes a champion more than any other thing: hating to fail and hating to not exceed your goals.

Back then, I had never even heard of the Olympics. Success and failure weren't tied to the Games but to my own personal accomplishments and mistakes. Think about it . . . in those days, there were only a few professional sportswomen in the entire world, and I didn't know about them because my government strictly monitored what we saw on television. Messing up at a competition didn't mean you weren't going to qualify for the next one. All it meant was that you hadn't done well and that you needed to improve. I never wanted to hear that I was incredible or perfect. I wanted to know I had talent, that I learned skills faster than the next girl, and that I was pretty good at my sport. That wasn't possible after my first Nationals.

Marta was fuming when I finished my beam routine. She believed in discipline, and she was terribly demanding. It was not enough to just do a skill: We had to do it correctly, or it was a waste of time. Marta also believed there must be mastery over the basics, which are truly the most important building blocks of a gymnastics career. The basics include strength, conditioning, and the perfection of the easiest of skills so that the more difficult ones are built upon a rock-solid foundation. A gymnast cannot do a flip on the beam unless the leaps and steps before that skill are so smooth that she will be perfectly positioned and balanced for the more difficult elements. Without the basics, a gymnast gets into dangerous accidents—rips muscles, breaks bones, cracks vertebrae. In my life, I have never seen another beam coach who has Marta's dedication to detail or who produces such incredible results in her gymnasts.

The Karolyis understood that, as children, we young gymnasts were incapable of disciplining ourselves, so they had to do it for us. They told us how many hours to practice (ranging from four to six a day) and how long to study (which was always as much as necessary to finish our work). Every night, we slept eight to ten hours so that our minds and bodies could be fresh. And each meal included specific portions of meat, vegetables, and milk so that our bodies and bones would grow stronger. Some kids hate being told exactly what to do down to putting out the light at night, but as a little kid, I didn't mind. I wanted to do everything Bela and Marta said because I wanted to be better; because I craved organization; and because, from early on, I was the leader of my group of little girls and felt I should be their role model.

But conditioning the body and the mind are two different things, and at age nine, my mind wasn't a steel-tight drum. What Marta didn't understand that day when I fell off the beam was that no matter what she said to me, I said worse to myself. I was frustrated, furious, humiliated, and determined to never have those kinds of mistakes plague me again. I came in thirteenth at that competition. In the end, my low score on the beam actually won the competition for our team, but I still felt miserable. I'd disappointed everyone, especially myself.

You asked in your last letter if I ever wanted to quit gymnastics, and that's a fair question. The answer is, never in the early days. Never. Gymnastics was fun. Bela had a vision of bringing all his experience in boxing, rugby, handball, and general athletics to gymnastics. He believed we could have the team spirit of rugby players, the toughness of boxers, and the aggression of handball players as well as all-around strength. Due to his size, he was a great spotter, and out of that grew respect and trust. The spotter is the person who keeps a gymnast learning new skills from getting hurt. If a gymnast knows that his or her spotter is dependable, that gymnast will have the courage to try more and more difficult skills without fear. With Bela, I always knew he wouldn't let me hit the ground or an apparatus. Plus, his attitude was light and easy compared to Marta's, so I really enjoyed working with him. Later, though, our relationship would change.

But I am getting ahead of myself. On the heels of failure came my first success, at the 1972 Friendship Cup. Our team's gymnasts were only ten years old. All the gymnasts from the other countries were in their late teens and early twenties. Bela and Marta hadn't even known how much younger we were before we arrived at the competition because they'd never seen the Soviet gymnasts, let alone the Czechs or Germans, compete. We walked into the arena, tiny little girls with pigtails, facing the likes of Lyudmila Turischeva, a long-legged and unbelievably graceful gymnast from Russia.

Today, Bela says that he always had a theory about copying. He explains that if, as a coach, you copy the style and training of the best gymnasts, your own gymnasts will never be as good—they'll be almost as good but not quite there. They will run behind but never catch up. If, however, you create gymnasts with unique styles, they will have a chance to outshine all others. I believe Bela's theory is true in life, too. Trying to be someone else may get you through the door, but being unique will get you noticed!

The Friendship Cup competition pitted the little girls against the big girls. We weren't as seasoned as some of the Czechs and Germans. Most of us had been training for years but had not been in as many competitions as gymnasts such as Tourischeva. But we concentrated and fell back on all the practice, training, and emotionally and physically demanding hard work we'd put in, and we exploded like fireworks. As a result of our conditioning, we had fantastic power and technique and performed skills never seen in gymnasts so young.

Bela and Marta had trained us to be professional regardless of the level of competition. We were so used to our busy routine during meets—stretching, visualizing each event, performing, and helping teammates prepare by measuring the location of the springboard for vaults—that we didn't have time to get nervous about the more experienced competitors. In the end, I won the all-around gold at the Friendship Cup. The team won the silver. We had done the unthinkable, beating the best international gymnasts in the world.

For me, winning has never been about standing up on a podium and having a medal draped around my neck. I used to look out at the audience and see all the people clapping; I watched Bela and Marta's smiles; I kissed the cheeks of my fellow competitors . . . but the drums inside me thrummed to a different beat. Standing up there, watching my country's flag rise, I felt pride, but even at a young age, my mind always replayed my performance and looked for holes, mistakes, opportunities to do better.

My friend, you think it is all about glory, but you are wrong. Winning is intensely personal in a way that might not make sense to you. What did I know about glory when I was ten? To me, competing was about the next time and the next and then the one after that. It was about improving my body and mind—overcoming frustrations, anger, and jealousy so that, in one shining moment, my body became a tool driven by unwavering concentration and desire.

After the Friendship Cup, my goal was simply to improve as a gymnast. For the next three years, there was nothing I wouldn't try, and I grew stronger, more focused, and more powerful with each day, month, and year. That is not to say that I didn't have setbacks or difficulties learning new skills or that I won every competition. But there was nothing I didn't want to learn, and that set me free to accomplish my goal. The power of a youngster is a thousand times stronger than that of an adult because there are no perceived boundaries for the child. I will tell you the story of the 1975 European Championships in Norway and let you see for yourself.

Originally, the Romanian Gymnastics Federation did not plan to send any of the Onesti gymnasts to the European Championships in Norway. There was another gymnastics club in Romania called Club Dinamo, which had a lot of money behind it and, consequently, a great program and very talented gymnasts. The federation usually chose Dinamo's gymnasts (because they had a history of good results) for important competitions, even after our school's girls began to shine brighter than theirs. When it was announced that three gymnasts would compete in Norway, all three came from Club Dinamo.

Bela refused to accept the federation's initial decision: The championship was too important. Only one year before the Olympics, it was an opportunity to attract international attention, which is vital if a gymnast wants to be scored to her fullest potential. Only gymnasts who make names for themselves garner enough attention to impress upon the judges that they are worthy of watching and of receiving high scores and even medals. Think about Olympic figure skating. I imagine that you recognize the names of the top three women in that sport. Medal-winning athletes just don't appear out of thin air; they are written and read about and watched. That is not to say that the athletes who receive the most attention aren't the best in their sports, but being a great athlete will not bring medals unless you are also noticed by the world.

In 1975, Bela turned to officials at the Ministry of Education (which funded our school), and together, they figured out a way to get one of the gymnasts from our team to Norway—they created an alternate position. That meant three girls from Dinamo and one of us would be sent. But who was going to go? This is where frustration and jealousy and the power of a child to master her emotions come into play. In 1975, Dorina was the best gymnast on our team. She had joined our school months earlier, and I immediately knew that she was good, very good. We became friends, but we were also rivals. Bela purposefully put Dorina and me together during practices, trips, and meets because he realized we both liked the competition and that it fueled us.

The day Bela announced that we'd have an interclub meet to decide which of his gymnasts would attend the European Championships, I knew the choice was between Dorina and me. All I can say is that on that day, I truly began to fly as a gymnast. Despite the fact that Bela was almost certain Dorina would win and consequently be the one attending the competition, I was in great form that day. The result was that I was chosen to attend the championships.

Many people have criticized Bela Karolyi and his style over the past decades. But I have never known a coach who fought harder—or more loudly—for his gymnasts' rights. There have been times when he has tap-danced along the gray line between right and wrong, fairness and injustice, but to know as a child that he is in your corner and to feel the warmth of his smile and praise is unlike anything else I have ever experienced.

Bela was in rare form at the European Championships. When Club Dinamo decided they'd only use two of their three gymnasts for the competition, Bela attained the unfilled third spot for me. I went on to win four gold medals, including the all-around European title. Lyudmila Turischeva, the current world and Olympic champion, was beaten by a little girl who had put aside every negative emotion and simply concentrated on being her best. I was not lucky. No one can be that lucky in gymnastics. You have skills that you're capable of doing, and you always know what you can and cannot deliver. If Marta were to say to me that I should do something a different way and I couldn't do it in practice, then I wouldn't be able to do it in a competition. Nothing fell out of the sky and touched me like magic as I swung from the bars or vault. Just as in life, everyone has things they can accomplish, and you put your skills in your bag and pull them out when needed. If they're not in your bag, you can't pull them out because you simply don't have them. The only pressure comes from losing concentration and slipping, not from performing skills you know you can deliver.

I've always been tough on myself about mistakes. As a child, I used to take chances and risks, but I won't anymore. I play the safe side of things now. Maybe that just comes with age. I think mistakes are a waste of time, but when I was younger, I believed that I had to learn by knocking my nose against the wall so I could tell the difference between good and bad by myself: I had a lot of bloody noses back then. But I digress and will tell you more about those mistakes later, if you are interested. First, let me get back to Ludmila.

I will never forget Ludmila's poise in defeat when she walked over to me at the championships and kissed me on the cheek. I still have the photograph of that moment because she was my idol. We couldn't communicate—we didn't speak the same language—but in that instant, I knew that she was a true champion and that I wanted to take some of her grace and make it my own. I believe you can take the attributes you admire in others and incorporate them into your own life. You can't copy someone else's gymnastics style and come out on top, but you can make yourself a better person by learning from another's actions.

In retrospect, I realize just how terribly disappointed Lyudmila must have been because the European Championships only happen every two years and she had won in 1971 and 1973. If she won in 1975, she would have been given the Challenge Cup for winning three times in a row. Later, I would be the first gymnast in the world to accomplish that feat—in 1975, 1977, and 1979—and to receive the Challenge Cup. But back then, I knew only that I was happy and that I hoped the Romanian people could share in my achievements. Still, I thought the European Championships were something important but small, like getting a 10 on a mathematics test at school (a perfect score in the Romanian grading system). There was no media attention on me until 1976, when the walls of my tiny world were blown apart and spotlights and camera flashes left me stunned like a deer in the road.

Dear friend, of course you have asked me about the 1976 Olympics. I had hoped you might be interested more in who I am now, and I'm tempted to give stock answers to a question that never seems to be put to rest—a question that has, at times, plagued me because I am no longer that tiny little girl with a brown ponytail in a snow-white leotard with red, yellow, and blue piping. I'm not sure I ever even knew her all that well.

You want me to remember every leap, somersault, and dismount from a time in my life that I thought was just another competition and that even now I find hard to put into historical context or perspective. I am not angered by your question but by my own confounding and complex feelings on the subject. And in truth, to know who I am now is to understand 1976 and what happened during and after that fateful Olympic year.

Do not think I fashion myself a victim, unless it is a victim of good fortune. But I am older and wiser, and I understand that with fame comes a sea of responsibilities that a young child must swim through. Sometimes, I felt myself sink beneath the surface of the water, and though I always struggled to rise and breathe, there were precious seconds when, I must confess, I just wanted to embrace the cold darkness.

How can I begin to explain that time? I will pull out a dusty copy of Jean Ure's book, *Romanian Folk Tales,* and turn to my favorite story, "Necessity." After you have read it, I'll attempt to shed some light on an Olympics that the world seems to recall better than the girl who held the spotlight and never quite escaped its glare.

Once there was a man. He had only one son by the grace of God, upstanding and handsome as a peony flower, but not knowing much about hardships as our man was well off.

This man wanted his son to learn to deal with difficulties and to look after the farm, so he sent him into the forest one day to get wood in a rather rickety old cart. "Now remember, lad, the cart's not very strong but if it breaks down you'll find necessity will teach you what to do."

The boy set off to get the wood with the idea that necessity was an old workman who lived in the forest and who helped people who had breakdowns.

When he got to the forest he loaded a fine cartful of wood and after he had had a bit of lunch he harnessed his oxen to the yoke and set off slowly home. They came to a rough place and the front axle broke right in two. He pushed it up and twisted it down but he just couldn't fix it in place again.

He remembered what his father had told him and climbed up on to a little mound and shouted at the top of his voice, "Ne . . . cess . . . ity . . . Ho there . . . ho . . . "

From another part of the wood he heard an answering shout: "'Ho there . . ." He ran toward it, thinking that he would find Necessity and that he would repair his cart. But he didn't find anybody.

He thought that he had somehow missed Necessity and shouted again till the valleys rang. He got the same answer.

Then our lad saw that evening was not far off and ran in the direction that the answer came from. He didn't find anybody that time either.

He tried a third time and then realized that necessity was not going to come and help him mend his cart. So he said bitterly, "What's the use of running round to get someone to work for me if it's likely to get dark while I'm still here?"

And with that he took his coat off and unloaded the cart, took a bit of wood the right length and in the twinkling of an eye the axle was ready and in place. He loaded the cart up again, yoked the oxen and by the time that day was giving place to night he was home.

His father came up to the cart and saw that it had a new axle. He asked the lad who had fixed it. The boy told him everything from beginning to end, and the father laughed and said, "Remember, my lad, that necessity is the best teacher."

Necessity is what you do in life when there is only one path, choice, or desire. Necessity is synonymous with need, requirement, inevitability, stipulation, and obligation. But at the 1976 Olympics, necessity for me meant only listening to Bela and Marta Karolyi.

The Romanian government used to pour money into its Olympic programs because our leaders believed that athletes represented the power of the government and validated our way of life. As a result, the infighting for individual athletes' rights to comprise their respective Olympic teams was fierce. Gymnastics was no exception, and because successful athletes generated privileges for each gymnast, their families, and especially the coaches, the pressure was unbelievable. Although our Onesti school's gymnasts had proven their worth, taking the top six places at the Romanian National Championships, Bela recalls that the federation still chose four gymnasts from Club Dinamo and only three from our school to be on the Olympic team.

"We have the right to compete as a team!" Bela told the government officials. "Nadia Comaneci is the European champion; the rest of the team has beaten every other gymnast in our country," he declared. "We won the Nationals!" In the end, it was decided that there would be a final competition in Bucharest—Onesti versus Dinamo. Bela moved our team to Bucharest. The summer was incredibly hot, but we practiced day in, day out, regardless of the heat. Club Dinamo's coaches took the weather into account and on particularly hot days allowed their gymnasts to go to the beach. I remember how jealous I was that Dinamo's gymnasts were given vacation days. I could taste that jealousy like the salty sweat that covered my skin and never dried.

One particularly sweltering afternoon, the general in charge of sports in Romania surprised us at the gym with a visit. As we dragged ourselves through our full routines, Bela and the man chatted, until the general asked where Dinamo's girls were. Bela replied, "At the beach." The general was furious that Dinamo's gymnasts weren't practicing and called for a meeting of both teams the following morning. When Dinamo's head coach couldn't make him understand that his gymnasts had needed some time to cool off, the general made Bela the head coach for the Nationals and the Olympic team. He now had the power to choose all the gymnasts. After watching both teams practice for another week, Bela made his decision. He took six gymnasts from our school and two alternates from Dinamo to the 1976 Olympics in Montreal, Canada. It was actually a fair decision on his part—our gymnasts were leaps above Dinamo's.

Friend, I need to put things into perspective for you because you are under the illusion that the Romanian team, myself included, thought that the Olympics were the biggest event in our lives. That was not the case. Until 1976, I believed that the European Championships were the most important gymnastics competition in the world. Everything I knew came from what I was told by my coach and my government. I'd never watched the Olympics on television, let alone televised gymnastics competitions from around the world.

So when I arrived in Montreal for the 1976 Games, I was flabbergasted. The Olympic Village blew my mind—its size and the number of security officials, coaches, and, above all else, athletes in more sports than I'd ever heard of. What I remember most was that everything—*everything*—was free. You were given a badge, and with it, you could see movies in the village's theater; you could get a soft drink; and you were given matching clothing, bags, hats, and pins. To me, it was so high-tech, so strange and exciting and absolutely wonderful. That first day, I was afraid to close my eyes because I didn't want to miss anything. Little did I know then that missing everything was part of the Karolyis plan to protect their gymnasts.

The men's and women's residences were separate, so Bela couldn't monitor us at night, but Marta was more than effective. We were not allowed to go anywhere alone. Everything was scheduled for us—breakfast at 7:00 A.M., training, rest time, lunch, and so on. We had a doctor traveling with the team, and he made sure we didn't try any food other than what we knew—meat, salad, nothing fancy. I saw, for the first time in my life, pizza, cottage cheese, peanut butter, and breakfast cereal. The smells of the cafeteria were overwhelming.

The Olympic Village, after my initial awe, became like anywhere else the team had traveled. We were just in another venue to have another competition. We did not march in the opening ceremony because Bela didn't feel comfortable having us stand on our feet for six hours with competition beginning the next day. I must admit that I agreed with his decision about the ceremony and virtually everything else during the Games. I didn't want anything—not food or late nights or catching a cold—to interfere with my ability to perform. Later, as I grew older and more independent, I would clash with the Karolyis' total control over my life, but I will never argue that in the early days, their style worked for me and helped me become a great gymnast.

You ask what my dreams were, going into the Olympics. When the media asked me the same question, I said the obvious, "I hope I'm going to win a medal." It was a reasonable dream in my mind, not an unbelievably audacious statement. I wanted to compete and do my job well, and I would have been happy with whatever color medal I received. I was not at the Olympics to be in a frenzy of grabbing gold medals. Everybody thinks of gold only, but if you win a bronze by moving from sixth place to third, that's success. I have always appreciated every medal I have won in that way. If I do my job and receive silver, then that's what I deserved. If I want more than that, then I should be better.

Of course, Bela and Marta's dreams were different from mine going into the Games. As adults, seeing their gymnasts with so many abilities, they wanted us to live up to our potential and to reflect their own talent. Show me fifty kids in a gym, and I can pick out the one or two with talent, which means they have incredible flexibility, balance, desire, and something magic that is indefinable and very rare. The Karolyis did that with thousands of kids and winnowed them down to the team from Onesti at the 1976 Games. They had a lot riding on their choices and decisions. The government had been generous and at times supportive of their experimental school. It was time for Bela and Marta to show their worth if they were to garner continued support. That meant we had to perform to our potential.

For me, I guess, my personal goal for 1976, which I did not share with anyone, was to create my own dream. I had no one to follow—my parents were not athletes, so I wasn't walking in their footsteps. My dream was to discover myself, to know what I could do, to push myself, and to be better than anybody else. You probably want to know why. But I don't have a good answer to what created my desires. It's just the way I am.

My first goal at the Olympics was to perform my podium workout well (this is the workout held in front of judges before the competition), so that I didn't bring any training mistakes into the real competition. When I was younger, Bela always used to tell me to pay attention to specific things during each routine, such as hand movements, certain skills, or inflections in the music. By 1976, he had stopped doing this because he finally realized that when he told me to pay attention to one thing, I'd make a mistake on something else. What I needed to pay attention to was vastly different from what he imagined. He was just creating more problems for me. But, to give Bela his due, at the 1976 Olympics he also created an environment in which I could shine. As I've tried to explain, the media, fans, and judges must notice athletes in order for those athletes to rate scores that will place them on the podium. Some coaches are just coaches. Other coaches, like Bela, are coaches, publicists, agents, and defenders all rolled into one. If an athlete is very talented and lucky enough to have a coach such as Bela, she has a better chance of thriving in the world of competitive athletics because she can focus on her sport and leave the politics to her coach.

What did you mean in your last letter when you said that I "came into my own" in 1976? I did not materialize at age fourteen at the 1976 Games. Gymnasts don't become great in a single year, just as actors never have "overnight successes" but instead work decades at their craft before their "big break." I was already a great gymnast by 1976, but no one knew that in the United States or Canada. Bela understood that nobody knew me or the Romanian team. Everyone expected great things from the Soviet and German gymnasts—athletes such as Olga Korbut and Ludmila Tourischeva. We, however, were from a tiny country no one could even find on the map. So Bela devised a scheme to focus the world's attention on his little girls.

The podium workout is an opportunity for all gymnasts to perform their routines on the actual apparatus used in the Olympics and in the gym where the competition will be held. Each team is given twenty minutes per apparatus, and most gymnasts perform watered-down routines so that they can avoid last-minute injuries brought on by nerves. The stands are filled with members of the media, fans, and judges. I have already told you that judges who do not recognize gymnasts tend to score them lower than the well-known girls. In 1976, the Romanian team was completely unknown, and Bela knew that had to change if we were to have a chance of winning.

"Now entering the arena for the 1976 Olympics, the team from Romania." I heard the loudspeakers blaring our country's name again and again and a light smattering of polite applause. It was time to enter the gymnasium for our podium workout, but Bela held us in the tunnel that led to the arena, not allowing us to enter. We were all dressed alike and wearing ponytails. Bela instructed us to march into the arena like soldiers and to perform our full routines with no mistakes. The loudspeaker blared our country's name again. "Mr. Professor, they're calling us," I ventured. Bela said to let them wait. When we finally entered the gym, the entire audience was watching the doors because we'd repeatedly failed to walk through them when called. The applause was a bit louder, and I could feel thousands of eyes watching us.

We were a curiosity, if nothing else. We were really tiny compared to the other gymnasts (most were in their late teens and twenties) and wore matching leotards. Gymnasts from other countries wore mismatched clothing and moved casually from apparatus to apparatus. Not us. Without ever sitting down, we ran through our routines, and we were flawless. By the time I dismounted the beam, the coaches, other gymnasts, and official delegates were in an uproar. The next day, the previously unknown team from Romania had to hide from reporters.

Friend, you wrote that I was an "automaton in '76, a tiny robot doing what everyone else wished." You are wrong. It is true that children do not choose their own paths at age six. What do they know? Parents clothe and feed them and decide when it is time for naps and bed. Parents pick their music, exercise, and outings. I was placed in a gym to play—that's all it was in my mind—and if I hadn't wanted to, I could have gone home. You cannot force a child to do anything as complex as gymnastics and to improve at the task unless that child wants to. I was given the chance to run, climb, jump, and soar, and I loved it from the moment I entered the gym. By age fourteen, when I reached the 1976 Games, I had already chosen my path; I was doing exactly as I wished.

The Karolyis and my government gave me an opportunity that my family never could have afforded. In other countries, you have to pay for your coach; for your private-school tuition; and for all of the leotards, wrist guards, shoes, and medical attention necessary for success. Things were different in Romania. My parents and my brother never suffered as a result of my desires. They could enjoy my successes while pursuing their own lives. In Romania, it was a big deal, a huge honor, to make it onto an elite athletic team. You were allowed to travel, and none of us could have afforded that. As a thirteen- or fourteen-year-old, you got to see other countries and buy stupid things that seemed really important at the time, such as dolls and ribbons and socks. Although I didn't understand the importance of the Olympics in 1976, I was a willing participant. I had the choice to participate, and I grabbed the opportunity with both hands and held on as tightly as humanly possible.

When the Romanian team entered the arena in Montreal for the Olympic compulsory competition, with our hair in ponytails and wearing snow-white leotards with striped piping, we were no longer the unknown team from a tiny country who-knows-where. There was a buzz, created by an unparalleled public relations move by Bela. Though many of the judges came from the USSR and favored the Soviets, our team dominated the compulsories; when I stepped up to the bars, we were in second place, only one-hundredth of a point behind the Russians.

No one knows when he or she is about to make history. There is no warning and no instruction manual on how to handle the moment. I can only tell you that it was business as usual as I swung onto the uneven bars. I executed each skill with the extension and movements expected of me, and I dismounted. I'd done the same compulsory routine as everyone else, but with a "Nadia touch." I felt an almost invisible hop on the landing but knew that my routine was good enough. It wasn't perfect, though.

Since I was the last to perform on the bars, I immediately went over to warm up for the beam. I never analyzed my performance beyond a quick thought of the landing. It was done, and I needed to move on. I knew that after the day was over, the Karolyis and I would talk about what I had done right and wrong. That's how we always processed competitions. While I warmed up for the beam, my score for the bars flashed across the scoreboard—a 1.00. I continued to warm up, unaware of what was happening, focused on my next routine. The crowd was silent, confused. No one knew what 1.00 meant.

Bela gestured to the judges to ask what my score meant, ready for a fight. A Swedish judge held up ten fingers. The reason my score had shown as 1.00 was that the scoreboard didn't have the programmed ability to flash a 10 because the organizers had never had the need for one before. Bela came over to me, and I asked, "Mr. Professor, was that really a 10?" He grinned from ear to ear and said yes. I've told you, friend, it is rare for me to show emotion on the outside, but I did smile then, and when one of my teammates told me to go up and wave to the crowd, I did that, too.

Promptly, I forgot about the 10 and moved on to the beam. During the rest of the competition, I got six more perfect scores of 10, for a total of seven at the Montreal Games. It didn't have an impact on me—not one bit. I thought that maybe the judges were being too good to me. The team was happy about my scores, but none of us focused on them. We needed to pay attention to the rest of the competition. I have always been able to concentrate. When I'm on the beam, I don't hear the music from the floor. And when I'm vaulting, I can't hear the applause when other gymnasts do their dismounts.

I do remember thinking at the time that I was glad to get a perfect 10 on the bars first because when I began gymnastics, bars were my original favorite. I loved the precision, the angles, and the complexity. Bars require a lot of thinking and figuring things out by using specific lines and points for reference. The Comaneci Salto and Comaneci Dismount that I performed during the 1976 Games came from countless hours of practice and thousands of falls. The idea that Bela and I had created new skills never seen before was exciting. But other than those random thoughts, receiving the first 10 for my uneven bar routine did not affect me. My fellow gymnasts were still my friends—my sisters. There was little personal jealousy because everything we did was de-signed to help the team, which benefited everyone. Bela was responsible for the strategy, and we were responsible for the consistency of our performances.

In the end, I won the all-around gold medal as well as an individual gold on bars and beam and a bronze on floor . . . and made history. Does this sound anticlimac-tic? Well, in a way, that's how it felt. There were a few moments of disbelief coupled with winning medals, which felt great, but as I've said, doing well was expected of me. It was my job. I accomplished my goals, every-one's goals, but winning a competition wasn't an enor-mous surprise. Very simply, that is what I was supposed to do. My moments of success felt incredible, but they were topped off by exhaustion and the desire to return home to my family and life.

There were no appearances on David Letterman or Oprah Winfrey. I didn't do a photo shoot for the cover of a magazine. Sports agents at IMG and CAA never beat down my door; they didn't even knock. I came, per-formed, made my country proud, and left the arena via a bus, not a limousine. I felt a sense of accomplishment, but there was practice, training, and more competitions ahead. The Olympics were over, and I was naive enough to believe I would never look back.

Nothing, my friend, is ever what it seems.

The Disciplined Life

My favorite vault as a competitive gymnast was the "Tsuka-hara." In this vault, a gymnast runs forward, springs off the springboard, and dives onto the horse with a one-half turn onto her hands, then performs a piked one-and-one-half somersault off the horse and lands facing it. The Tsukahara was the first multiple-flipping vault for women. Before that, gymnasts performed a variation of a handspring over the vault. The Tsukahara was much more difficult and dangerous than any other vault, and that's why I liked it. I always wanted to do the hardest skills possible. I was one of a handful of gymnasts who did a Tsukahara, and some experts thought I performed it better than anyone, including the guy who invented it.

During the 1976 Olympics, I did not realize how much media attention was focused on the Romanian team or me. We didn't watch television or speak to other athletes, so there was no way to know. Plus, the media were not allowed into the Olympic Village, so we had no contact with reporters and journalists. But Bela and

Marta knew, and they asked the Romanian government to allow us to go home immediately after the Games. They found the attention overwhelming and frightening and wanted to make certain the team was safe. There was no immediate flight, so we were taken to a youth camp in Canada, which was a treat. I was still under the impression that I'd done very well at the Olympics but not that I had become a national figure or a heroine back in my country.

Friend, I understand the curiosity in your last letter about our return to Bucharest. You've watched countless athletes return victorious to your own country, and there is an expectation for ticker-tape parades, speeches, and screaming fans. Until 1976, that had never happened in our country, so how was I to know or be prepared for what lay ahead? When our plane landed in Bucharest, I still had no clue. I stepped out the door and down the stairs, and the thousands of Romanians who had come to meet our plane overwhelmed me. We'd gone to countless important competitions before, but never had we been met by cheering fans or had Nicolae Ceausescu order a celebration for our arrival. I recall that I had been carrying a doll in my hands and that I was crying because I had lost it after somebody pulled on her leg. It was scary—all those years when nobody cared and now, suddenly, everyone was pushing, pulling, and trying to touch me.

We were taken to an awards ceremony, and Ceausescu personally gave out Romanian government awards to the Karolyis and the gymnasts. I had never met Ceausescu before, and it was like meeting the president of the United States. It was an honor for a kid, a big deal. Politics back then was a different world, and I had nothing to do with it.

So, you want to know what changed. Nothing . . . at first. I went back to Onesti and back to the experimental school, classes, and practices. My father still didn't have a car; my mother was still a homemaker. I received a monetary award from my government for my medals but nothing too big; after all, I lived in a Communist country. I was also still receiving a monthly stipend from the government for being an elite gymnast, but my mother was in charge of all that money. I'm lucky that she saved it because in the end, I desperately needed what she put away for me.

Please don't assume, like everyone else does, that when I won the 1976 all-around gold medal I became a wealthy girl. Perhaps you've heard rumors, but our country was closed to foreign journalists, and the only information that got out to the world was what my government chose to share. Sometimes it was the truth, but more often than not it was self-serving. I still lived in a simple dormitory a few minutes from home. I returned every weekend to my family's house, but in truth, I was bored there because at the dorms, I had twenty other girls to play with. And at home, my mother still made me do the dishes.

There was no time to rest on my laurels. No one is selected off the streets for the Olympics. You work your way up to it. Despite what my mother and I originally may have thought, gymnastics was not exactly a hobby for me. Not if I wanted to succeed, avoid injuries, and be the best in the world. Plus, Bela was not the kind of guy who would tell me that I was perfect. He always said I could do better, and I lived under that. He never put too much emphasis on those times when I did something great. It was always about the next time.

So when I returned to school, I still woke up every morning and had breakfast at 7:00 A.M. and then went to the first training session from 8:00 until 11:00. I went to classes from 11:00 until 2:00 P.M., rested for a few hours, and then headed back to the gym for late practice until 7:30. We ate dinner after our second practice, did homework, and then had lights out by 10:00 P.M.

Our meals were all very regimented—mostly grilled meat, fish, and salads and fruit. We didn't eat any pastas or bread because the team doctor didn't believe they were important components of a well-balanced meal. The doctor designed a menu based on what each week demanded nutritionally, such as protein, vegetables, fruit, and milk. Meals were not about enjoyment but about nutrients. You ate what was on your plate, whether you liked it or not. There were a few exceptions. I liked fried cheese, and the team doctor let me have it once a week. We all loved chocolate and were given a piece each day before training because the doctor believed it gave us energy. To this day, I love chocolate—probably because I was only allowed to have a little of it as a child.

You asked in your last letter if the rumors about Bela Karolyi's cruelty as a coach were true. I want to try to put that question into perspective by asking *you* a few questions. How much can you really understand of a man who struggled to survive under Ceausescu's regime? Who defected with his wife but was forced to leave his daughter behind, with the knowledge that it might take years to get her out of Romania? Can you comprehend what it takes to help a young girl recognize her potential and then live up to her dreams . . . dreams that are enormous and beyond the reach of almost anyone in the world? How much can *I* really understand Bela, for that matter? I can only tell you what I perceived then and what I believe today. You will have to make your own judgment on this subject.

Bela Karolyi is a great coach; he is a masterful motivator and a powerful man who is as complex as any human being. I do not know the details of his coaching relationships with other gymnasts, but I do know that he is a good person. He motivated me as well as the rest of our team by the sheer force of his personality, which could be incredibly fun and animated when we tried our best or disappointed and somber when we failed him and ourselves. Because we all knew that Bela was a skilled coach and a fair man, we took his coaching very seriously. But Bela also understood how to read our emotions, and when he sensed we were tired, he'd devise countless games that combined fun with the conditioning exercises we still needed to do to complete our workouts. We'd have races while doing backbends or hold each other's feet in the air in a wheelbarrow position, using our arms to scamper across the floor exercise mat. Bela used fun, discipline, and our powerful desires and personalities in combination with his own to motivate us to strive for success.

Bela and I did not always see eye to eye, and as I grew up, we needed time and distance to help us both deal with the changes that came. But he was never cruel to me. Fierce, yes; a tough disciplinarian, yes; and fair—always. Plus, he was funny. I know that when Bela came to the United States, he didn't speak the language. Maybe some of the things he said to his gymnasts then didn't quite translate into humor. But there's also a big difference between the cultures of Romania and America.

Four years after Bela arrived in the United States, he made Mary Lou Retton into a top-notch gymnast, and she won Olympic gold. For a little while, everyone thought Bela was great ... but happy endings are only interesting for a short time. It's controversy that sells. Bela single-handedly refashioned the U.S. system of gymnastics. In order to be competitive with the Soviets and Romanians, he told American girls that they had to practice six hours a day, not three. He would have loved to find a way for his gymnasts to work less and be that good. But it just wasn't possible. The secret of success was the three extra hours. Everyone started to do it, and everyone got better. For the first time in its history, the United States began winning gold medals—lots of gold medals. But when there is money to be made and when there are disappointed girls and parents, there is always the danger of being targeted by unhappy people. I'm not saying that Bela has always done the right thing, for it's impossible for a human being to be right all the time. But only he and the gymnasts in question know the truth of their situations. I was not there, so I can only tell you what I know of my old coach.

Bela always believed that if a kid didn't want to work as hard as was necessary to win, fine. But he wasn't going to waste his time on any gymnast who wasn't as committed as he was to achieving in the sport. What's wrong with that? If a child just wants to play, then enroll her in a gymnastic program that's designed for play. If she wants to shoot for the moon, then work with Bela. It takes a great coach to train a great gymnast, and not all coaches can work effectively with certain girls or boys. Finding the right coach who can bring out a child's motivation, fire, and desire is a difficult process. It's important for a coach to help an athlete work harder and improve if that's the ultimate goal. But in general, it's also important to have someone in your life who will challenge you to be your best. Bela did that for me, and I feel fortunate that our paths crossed.

To my knowledge, Bela has never forced a child to do anything. He says only that "this is the right way to do things." It has been documented that his style of training works. If parents don't like it, if it's wrong for their child, then they should lead that child in a direction more suited to his or her individual personality. I don't really understand all the hoopla that's ensued over the years about Bela's style. My friend, if you don't believe in Bela's way, then get a book about gymnastics and read it. There are no secrets. Back then, we didn't know too much, but everything is in black and white today. As for the gymnasts and parents who say that Bela was mean or that he called children names, what do I know of that? He treated me fairly, but it was a different time and place, and I was a driven young person. I trusted Bela with my life in the gym. He quite literally kept me from breaking my neck. And I trusted him with my career, too. Let me tell you a story that you may have heard a little about before.

Paris, France, 1974. The French government was holding a gymnastics demonstration, and officials there were in need of more gymnasts. They called our government, which in turn called Bela and ordered him to take two gymnasts to the prestigious event. Bela selected Dorina and me. Both of us were incredibly excited; we had never been to Paris. When we arrived at the airport in France, there was no one there to meet us. None of us spoke French or English, and Bela was forced to figure out a way to communicate in order to get us to the competition. With little time to spare, we finally found a driver and raced through winding streets and ran red lights to get to the arena on time. When we arrived, Bela left us in the car to make certain we were in the right place. We weren't.

The French had not expected Romania to send such young gymnasts, and believing we weren't capable of performing alongside gymnasts such as Lyudmila Turischeva, they sent us to a competition for younger girls. Bela was furious. He decided we'd participate in the smaller competition, but then he'd try to find a way into the one for seniors. In a small gymnasium that reeked of cigarette smoke, we performed our routines, then raced back to the car and charged to the other arena. Dorina and I thought at the time it was just a fun adventure, but Bela was dead serious.

We were barred at the entrance of the arena by security guards. While the interpreter tried to explain our presence, Bela grew impatient. He told us to stick close, and then he pushed his way through the barriers. We ran behind a stack of mats and hid. The exhibition was half over, and the gymnasts were performing their vaults. Ludmila was the last to vault, and as soon as she finished, Bela told me to run down to the floor of the arena and do a Tsukahara vault. There was no time to measure my run or where the springboard was positioned. He told me I could do it anyway, so I did. I had complete faith in him.

I performed a perfect vault. The confused exhibition officials located our interpreter and asked him to explain who we were and where we were from. When the people in the audience heard I was only twelve, they went crazy. Still, we were told not to interrupt the rest of the exhibition. Bela agreed, but when Lyudmila finished her beam routine, he sent me out again. The crowd once again was delighted, and the officials had no choice but to give permission for Dorina and me to perform a floor routine together. We dazzled everyone.

This story isn't just an example of Bela seizing the moment so that his gymnasts would be better known before the European Championships. It shows that I was willing to tune out the world and concentrate completely at Bela's request because, back then, I would have followed him through fire if he told me it would make me a better gymnast. No child could have believed so much in a man who was unfair or cruel.

Bela was a lot of things, though, and one of them was a believer in nontraditional medicine. I remember the time there was a flu going around our experimental school before a competition. He believed that if we ate raw garlic every day, we wouldn't get sick. We hated garlic because when we worked out and sweat, we smelled like hell. The weeks before the competition, we ate whole cloves of garlic every day, and Bela also had it put into our food like grated cheese. Raw garlic! We went to the competition without a single case of the flu on our team. Still, every day, Bela still made us eat garlic in case the gymnasts from other countries might have the same illness. Their coaches, curious about what we ate and how it helped us perform, began to copy our eating habits. Pretty soon, every gymnast in Europe was eating raw garlic. I remember saying to myself, *It's not the garlic, people, it's the training!* We simply worked harder.

We did work harder, even when we didn't recognize it as work. Bela knew me—he knew all his gymnasts so well. He could read everyone's body language without our saying a word. If we took fifty seconds to chalk up our hands before getting on the bars instead of the ten seconds it usually took, he knew we weren't ready to learn a new skill. He'd switch gears and devise exercises that would be fun but that would also help us move one step closer to performing whatever skill had initially frightened us.

When his gymnasts were ready to get on an apparatus and learn something new, Bela would always be there for us. He never—*never*—let us hit the ground. As I have said, what he expected in return was obedience. We had to be on time. On the dot. Infractions of the rule would result in being left home during competitions. We had to do the exact number of repetitions of each skill as asked. And when we were told to go to sleep, we were to immediately turn out the lights, cease talking, and, above all else, not jump on our beds.

I will never forget the one time Bela caught us up late, playing, jumping, and giggling. He came into our dorm seconds after we'd heard him and flicked the light off. "Your light was on," he said, smiling. We lied and disagreed. "You must not be sleepy. Maybe you need to get a bit more tired before you close your eyes." He took us outside in our pajamas and told us to start running. We were laughing and giggling though the whole punishment. But the next day, when we were expected to wake up early, practice, go to school, practice again, and do our homework, we were exhausted. I don't remember ever not turning out the lights on time again.

After 1976, Bela became even stricter. I believe it was extremely difficult for him to face the fact that we had reached our midteens. He became overprotective and, as I saw it, overbearing. He believed his gymnasts were being spoiled by attention, though I never really under-

stood why. I remember only that there was a lot of interest among the media about how we trained and what we
were allowed to do and why. Bela hated that.

I began to have disagreements and misunderstand-
ings with Bela by mid-1977. Just little things at first. I
was trying to stretch my wings and grow up, and like any
teenager, I had the desire and need to be on my own. I
saw girls my age dating, going to movies, driving cars. I
wanted those things, too. All of a sudden, there were
other attractions, and because I was sixteen and knew
that my career would end sooner, not later, my focus
drifted. Maybe, I thought, I was getting a little old for
this. I started going to practices late. Bela was completely unused to any defiance on my part. I always did
things by the book because I felt that was the only way to
improve.

Do not misunderstand me. I believe in the disciplined life—maybe too much so at times. It depends on
what kind of life you want to have, though, and what you
want to accomplish. Even today when I travel for work, I
accomplish my goals because of discipline. If I have a
2:00 P.M. press conference, I work backward and figure
out what I can get done before I have to shower, drive,
and arrive at the venue. I work things through down to
the smallest detail, such as when I can get in a thirty-
minute workout, how long it will take to shower, and
whether I have time for breakfast or if I should eat while
working. I can only give everyone the best of me if I am
carefully organized and scheduled. That is the disciplined life.

My parents were always disciplined, so I didn't just
learn that way of life from Bela and Marta. My father
worked every day and rarely took a sick day. My mother

was extremely organized and hated things to be out of place in her home. I took to their habits and was always incredibly neat. In school, I kept blue pens in one place, black in another. It sounds a little weird and compulsive, but to be "normal" and do normal things doesn't get you anywhere except normal. I always wanted to be extraordinary. My childhood showed me that discipline works—if I practiced, ate well, and turned off my lights at 10:00 P.M., I'd be rested and ready for the next day. It is a simple and good way to live.

Tough Teens

The most important part about the vault is the run. It's an 82-foot-long run to the springboard. Gymnasts don't count their steps but instead adjust them as they run so that they hit the springboard at the same spot each time they vault. Most elite gymnasts take the same number of steps every time they make their runs because those steps are ingrained in their minds and muscle memory.

A great vault is dependent upon the speed of a gymnast's run and her push-off from the vault. Without good speed, a vault requires much more effort to perform. Without enough push, it's hard to have the height and rotation needed for a good landing. The danger of not having enough speed or push is either landing on your head or underrotating and breaking your leg or jamming an ankle. I liked vaulting, but there were some days when I woke up and just didn't feel like running fast.

Becoming a teenager wasn't that simple, and neither were the 1977 Prague European Championships. First, they were televised in Romania, and after the Olympics, the country, including President Ceausescu, took a big interest in gymnastics. Second, the competition was very important to me because I was defending my title as the European champion. Third, the championships signaled the end of my childhood relationship with Bela and the beginning of a complex collaboration between a strong-willed young woman and her determined coaches.

The European Championships were different that year for a single reason—the advent of the perfect score. Before 1976, most gymnasts and their coaches didn't take as many risks or focus as much on the technical aspects of the sport. But by the 1977 European Championships, a new type of gymnast had emerged. She was smaller, younger, leaner, and focused not only on mastering technique but also on pushing the envelope on each apparatus to achieve the maximum level of difficulty and the highest possible score. Though this may have brought gymnasts to a higher level, it also meant that there was very little margin for error—if a gymnast made the slightest mistake, her chances of victory were dashed.

Despite the fact that I was the previous European champion or that I'd won the all-around gold at the Olympics, I faced tough competition. Yelena Mukhina was the newest member of the Soviet team, competing alongside Maria Filatova and Nelli Kim. Steffi Kraker, on the East German team, was also a strong rival. Friend, you asked about Elena and her accident in your letter, and I will tell you that story, but first let me finish writing about Prague because it is one of those times when you believe nothing will change in your life and then everything does.

The strange thing is that nothing before or during the Prague championships was out of the ordinary. The night before the competition began, Bela instructed all his gymnasts to go to bed early, to do what we'd learned in training, and to ignore the media and focus solely on our performances. The next morning, Dorina and I asked for instructions before the competition started. Bela told us that even with the higher standards, we both had a great chance if we did as we'd been told. And he said to me that he expected nothing less than complete sureness and concentration and would not accept failure of any sort, for there was no excuse for it. I agreed.

After the first day of competition, I had won the all-around, followed by Yelena in second and Nelli in third. But the apparatus finals changed everything. As I said, though, nothing was outwardly strange. As usual, Bela got frustrated by some of the scores and fought for his gymnasts—throwing his hands up in disgust whenever he thought the judges were unfair. These things happened during every competition. During the finals, both Nelli and I performed the vaults we were supposed to do with good results. Our final scores were added to our preliminary day's scores, and when the official board flashed, Nelli and I were tied for the gold on the vault. When we marched toward the podium to receive our medals, my name was called for the silver and Nelli's for the gold. Somehow, my score had been lowered. I don't know how, by whom, or why.

I turned my focus to the bars, competed, and received a 10 despite what had just happened on the vault. I moved on to the balance beam and performed another near perfect routine. After my dismount, Bela told the team members to pack our bags—we were leaving the arena before the end of the competition. A man from the Romanian embassy had told Bela that our government had ordered us to go home. I didn't want to leave: I wanted to compete because I'd spent countless hours in practice to do just that. But it didn't matter what I wanted. As I left the arena, I glanced back and saw my beam score. It was another 10.

A government official later explained the reason for having our team walk out of the competition. The entire country of Romania had been watching the championships, and the people were infuriated by the unfairness of the judges. For the first time in our country's history, the event had been on television, and when they'd seen Bela carrying on and shaking his fists against the judges, they demanded that the Romanian team be saved from injustice. What they didn't understand—and what I now understood completely—was that injustices were part of gymnastics, some big, some small, and some just a matter of perception. When we flew into the airport at Bucharest, there were enormous crowds and mass hysteria in support of our team. I felt torn in two— it's hard to know what to believe when you think one thing and your entire country thinks another.

You wanted to know what life was like after the 1976 Games, and I continue to disappoint you, dear friend. Where are the fairy-tale endings, the mansions, and money? Where is my sweet sixteen birthday party and dinners at Ceausescu's palace? They are the stuff of fantasies. In truth, after 1976, I began the sometimes troubling and difficult process of growing into a young adult in a Communist country.

Bela believed that the unbridled support of the nation would further erode his gymnasts' disciplined lives. I think, however, that the erosion was a by-product of our ages. We were older and smarter, and we finally understood that life and competition were never fair and that obeying was a choice, not a given. We were teenagers, and part of that meant expressing a level of defiance toward authority of any kind, feeling the desire to push our boundaries, and having the need to strive for independence. Except that, unlike "average" teens, we were also elite athletes, and to maintain our abilities, we still needed to follow a very regimented schedule.

The desire to be a teen clashed with the desire to be an elite athlete. It was a tough time, just as it is for any teen, whether he or she is a gymnast, plays high school soccer, or edits the school yearbook. The only way to get through those tough teen years is to get through them with as few regrets as possible. At the time, my mother told me that if I didn't want to train, I should just quit. Don't play around, was her message, but I wasn't really listening, though there were many wake-up calls.

Two years after Prague, Yelena Mukhina broke her neck during training. It was something that could have happened to any of us. I know you want to understand the accident because it scares you and you need a reason to explain it away, but I don't know what went wrong, only that Yelena got disoriented in midair and broke her neck when she hit the ground and was paralyzed. Believe me, all of us wanted to explain away what occurred because if Yelena, who was an elite gymnast with years of conditioning, could break her neck, then what about the rest of us? At the time, I accepted the accident as just an incredibly unlucky event.

My mother was right, though: Gymnastics wasn't a game to play around with—it was to be taken seriously or not at all. But still I dabbled because I was a teenager and believed I was invincible. It wasn't that I wanted to go to discos or late-night parties. I wasn't even particularly interested in dating. Back then, girls didn't start dating at twelve; they were eighteen before anything serious occurred. Plus, I'd spent my entire childhood and early teens with only girls. I wasn't sure how to act around boys, other than giggling, thinking they were cute, and maybe going out for a soda.

There weren't many people for me to talk to about how I was feeling. I've never had many friends. If I have one, a good one, that's enough. More than five, I always thought, was a waste of time. My brother was my best friend and confidant back then. It's very difficult to find real friends. I like people who are fair, realistic, and sincere and who tell me the truth. Otherwise, I don't consider them my friends. If I hear that something I've said has reached the wrong ears, I don't give too many second chances.

You might think that's excessively harsh, but remember, I'm from a country where people were told what to say and where two out of three citizens were members of the Securitate (the secret police) or informants of some sort. Life was hard in Romania, and people did what they had to in order to survive. It's hard for you to fathom, growing up in the United States where police don't bug your telephone or every room in your home. But I was considered a national treasure because I made my government's rule and way of life look good, and state officials were determined to protect that at all costs. Can you imagine such an existence?

In 1977, I didn't comprehend the extent of the danger around me; mostly, I was just trying to sort out what to do next. I felt as if my gymnastics career was coming to an end and that I should move to Bucharest and start taking college classes so I could figure out what I wanted to study. Like any teen, I felt confused and restless and ready for the next stage of my life. I'd worked so hard to be a great gymnast, but suddenly, it didn't feel like enough. My lack of desire to achieve and compete was so unlike me. I had always been focused on gymnastics and success. And I still believed in the value of sportsmanship, which included professionalism, respect for my teammates and coach, and holding myself to the highest standards. But I was exhausted from the competitions and media attention, and I just couldn't do what my coaches demanded or my gymnastics and my team required.

From what I understood at the time, the Gymnastics Federation decided that the best thing was to grant a "trial separation" between my coaches and me for a loosely defined period of time. The official reason for my split with the Karolyis was so that they could once again work as talent scouts and create a new training center in the village of Deva. I left for Bucharest, where I was told that I'd train and compete for a few more years but would have the opportunity to go to school. Meanwhile, Bela, who says he was never told that I was being moved, arrived one day for our regular training sessions to find me gone. He was devastated.

Once in Bucharest, I began to train at the 23rd August Sports Complex. My new coach was much more mellow. I played around a lot—went to the movies, the park, the discos. I'd sleep tons, watch TV, then go back to sleep. It was a very sedentary life. I tried all of the foods I'd never been allowed to eat—for example, ice cream. I liked the freedom of having no schedule, but I didn't truly enjoy the unorganized life. It made me feel slothful and uncertain. I was too young to get a job, and I had no skills. What was I going to do, work in a factory?

The next six months were lost time for me. Many teenagers go through a period like this, and it is very uncomfortable. I gained weight due to puberty and overeating. It was hard to see my body change. Plus, my parents were having difficulties in their marriage and decided to divorce. I worried about my dad, alone in the apartment where we were once a family. My mother had my brother with her. But my dad was by himself, and I missed him.

I believe a lot of children have similar feelings when their parents divorce: Whose fault is it? Will either parent be lonely? Will Mom or Dad ever meet someone else to marry? Will they feel lonely, sad, hurt? Will I be replaced by a new family or another daughter? The younger the child, the worse a divorce feels. It's important to remember that it's never your fault when your parents divorce because they're the adults and make the big decisions and you're just a kid. But despite the fact that I knew my parents' relationship problems were between them and had nothing to do with me, I was filled with anxiety and sadness as a result of the situation.

Friend, I do not blame you for the "big" question you asked in your letter. You're right to think I wouldn't like it, but it must be answered—not just for you or me but to set the record straight after so many untrue stories have been told. Yes, I was very unhappy in 1978. But no, I did not attempt suicide by drinking a bottle of bleach because I saw my boyfriend with another girl as the movie *Nadia* showed. I have heard many accounts of that day and what supposedly happened; some journals in

Germany even wrote that I drank two bottles of disinfectant because I was heartbroken at the breakup of an affair with a poet.

The truth is that I had been promised, both by my government and by my new coaches in Bucharest, that I'd be given more freedom while living at the 23rd August Sport Complex. On the day in question, a female official stopped me outside the door to my apartment. She asked where I was going. Annoyed, I told her I was going to get some detergent and bleach so I could do my laundry. I returned to my room, wrote a letter, and then left again to do my wash. There were now three officials outside my room. They were pretending to play cards, but they were there to watch me.

"Where are you going now, Nadia?" the officials innocently asked. I hit the roof. "What are you doing here?" I demanded. "Why can't I do laundry without the third degree? How can I feel relaxed when there are people ready to jump on me at every corner? Maybe," I said flippantly, "I should just drink this bottle of bleach and commit suicide. Please leave me alone!" I stalked back into my room and slammed the door. I hated being policed, scrutinized, and constantly watched, and I was fed up. From one comment made out of frustration, rumors and stories evolved, and to this day, some people believe I actually attempted suicide, which is ridiculous and completely untrue.

My gymnastics suffered from all of this drama and unhappiness, and by the time the Senior Nationals were held in Bucharest, I was not in physical or mental condition to compete. I watched from the bleachers. The Karolyis brought all of their new little gymnasts from Deva to the Nationals. After the compulsories, they held the first six places. After the optionals, they'd won them all.

As a result of his success, Bela was asked by the government to take the Senior Nationals team to the World Championships in Strasbourg—not his new little girls, who were in great shape, but the members of his previous team, all of whom had been leading a less disciplined existence and weren't ready for a World Championships competition. Bela tried to say no, but the government insisted that at least a few of the Nationals gymnasts be included on the team with the less experienced girls. He went to the complex to see me the next day.

When I opened the door of my room, Bela looked horrified. He had seen my face in the stands but hadn't been certain it was me. I had gained quite a bit of weight, and I was out of shape. He sat down, and we began to talk. He wasn't angry; he was nice and parental. I know that I cried, remembering the old days and my past glory. I rarely cry and never in front of people. If I cry, I do it alone because I don't want anyone to see me upset . . . so that day, I must have been *extremely* distressed.

"Do you think you can come back, Nadia?" Bela asked.

"I don't know—sometimes I want to, but sometimes I think I can't do it," I replied.

"Do you want to come back?"

Again, I was uncertain. "I like the end results," I explained, "but I don't know if I can get there."

He told me that it would be hard. Probably, he said, the hardest thing I'd ever do in my life. It would be incredibly difficult for me to regain my body, power, and skills, but he knew I could do it, Bela said. I agreed but added that if I couldn't give 100 percent, then it wouldn't work.

"Nadia, let me tell you what to expect before you make a final decision," Bela said. "If you come back with me, there is absolutely no way you will get out of going to the World Championships. The government wants you, more than anybody else, to compete in Strasbourg. Your conditioning will be the ultimate torture, and ready or not, you will have to go to those championships."

You asked me why I didn't just retire once I grew tired of gymnastics. Do you still not understand who I am? I don't give up, ever. I don't run away from a challenge because I am afraid. Instead, I run toward it because the only way to escape fear is to trample it beneath your feet.

■ The Scorpion

My individual uneven bar routine: Start facing the low bar. Jump with one half-turn; glide kip catch to the high bar. Cast to the Comaneci Salto, swing forward, and beat the low bar. Swing backward with a back uprise to a full twist. Catch the high bar immediately, transfer to the low bar, then glide kip low bar, forward hip circle, "Brause Salto" to high bar, catching it with a mixed grip. Immediate full twist, drop to low bar, glide kip, catch the high bar. Straddle over the low bar, and with hips on the low bar, kip up to the high bar to a cast handstand one-half pirouette. Beat the low bar back, uprise to a free hip, circle to handstand, then another free hip circle to a handstand to an immediate toe-on to a Comaneci Dismount.

───────

Friend, my 1978 decision to return to Deva was tougher than you might imagine. I had no one to help me make the choice. My mother always had a stock answer—"If you want to do it, do it. If not, quit." If she'd said otherwise, if she'd ever tried to push me, I would never have become a gymnast in the first place. That is the way I am. If someone tells me to do something, I won't do it. I firmly believe that if you do anything solely because somebody else wants you to do it, then things won't work out.

After weighing my decision and balancing out the pros and cons, I agreed to go to Deva on the condition that I no longer had to live in the dormitory with the younger gymnasts. The federation and Bela agreed to the compromise and got my mom and brother a temporary house nearby. It was small—only two rooms, with my brother and I sharing one—but it was ours. We got a dog, Becky, who was my tiny best friend. Being home with my family gave a balance to my life that I hadn't had before.

Bela was true to his word. My training was torture. Before dawn each day, we took a run, just Bela and me, and I wore lots of layers of clothing and did conditioning exercises while running. The following three hours were spent in the gym training, and afterward, I'd go for a second run, followed by a massage. After the rubdown, I did weight training, took a sauna, and did a shorter run. Bela was with me every moment. Most of the extra weight on my bones fell off, but I was exhausted. I'd roll out of the gym . . . I could hardly walk.

We didn't do much gymnastics at first because Bela didn't feel comfortable having me try to perform skills when I wasn't conditioned. He was a stickler about that because with a different body, I might have hurt myself. I sucked it up and did everything as he instructed; it was like the old days. My meals consisted of salads and fruits at first—nothing else. I craved everything that was bad for me. And unlike the old days, I now knew what ice cream and other desserts tasted like. For the first few weeks, I had to stay at Bela and Marta's home so that they could keep me under strict supervision. If they hadn't, I would have sneaked food.

I am not saying that my eating regimen during those first few weeks was right for anyone trying to get in shape or lose weight. You have to remember that I'd had years of healthy eating that had made my bones and body strong. A few weeks of lighter food couldn't hurt me. I realize that body misperceptions and eating disorders are an enormous problem for young girls, but I don't believe that depriving a body of the protein and fats it needs will help anyone achieve overall health. I am not a doctor, so I can't give much advice on this subject except to say that eating a balanced diet and getting exercise is the only way I know to maintain a healthy mind and body. Once Bela and Marta had gotten me back on track with my eating, I was permitted to live at home with my mother and brother, and I resumed following a well-balanced diet.

You asked if there were moments when I was ready to give up. Yes, there were, but Bela wouldn't let me. I had made a commitment to him and to myself, and he would see that I met it. Slowly, I started to dream more of my glory days, the Olympics, and other competitions. I began to dream about skills and realized that I missed being a great gymnast. I'd tried a "regular" life, and it wasn't for me. I wasn't happy being like everyone else. I missed the thing that made me special. When I moved to Bucharest, I'd never officially decided to retire; there was no big celebration for me or a huge reward. Instead, I'd halfheartedly continued training and disappeared through the back door. It was not a style that became me.

After the first few weeks of training, I wanted to be back on top. But as you pointed out in your last letter, it's easier said than done. Training, especially as an elite gymnast, is repetitive and at times boring, and it can be painful and frustrating. Mostly, it's a solitary endeavor. No matter how much support you're given from family, friends, and coaches, ultimately you have to succeed on your own. The only things that are concrete come from each individual. The power to make it to the top and stay there comes from within alone. I like challenges, the harder the better. I love being told something is impossible because I want to do what no one has ever done before. I long to be the groundbreaker.

My goals when I moved to Deva were clear. I wanted to get back to where I was before. It wasn't about the Worlds or the European Championships or the next Olympics. It was about proving that I could accomplish what the media and world thought was not possible. If I wanted to retire later, fine. But for the moment, I wanted to be the best again, period. So, 1978 was my year to return to reality, and it was a tough adjustment. I wasn't ready at the World Championships and struggled to finish my floor routine. Five weeks was not enough time to make up for a year without discipline. Bela believed that the competition would wake me up, motivate me, and show me the process I needed to complete to get back on top. He was right. The floor and bars were the worst because I simply couldn't carry any extra weight and be as good as I had been. It's hard enough to propel yourself through the air or hang from your arms when you're in perfect condition, but if you add pounds, tough skills become almost impossible because your timing and strength are off.

There were glimmers of the past, particularly on the beam, where I won a gold medal. The beam is an event that requires leg strength more than arm strength, and I still had the lower-body power. But I tasted humility at that competition and couldn't wait to get out of the arena. It was an experience I was determined to erase from my memory the moment it was over. I recognized that it was nobody's fault but mine; I'd created the situation with my own hands, and I would just have to live through it. That's the way I look at every episode in my life. The negatives are fleeting. Nothing is big enough to damage me. You've asked me how I could get through the tough spots, and my only answer is that I did it by imposing a perspective on the situation.

At the Worlds, Bela was pleased with the younger girls, who'd won four medals, and with my efforts. We heard that Ceausescu was very disappointed with the results of the competition (we didn't win) and by my own performance. It is so strange to think that the leader of my country watched gymnastics—let alone me—or that he cared how I did. Stranger still is to comprehend that he believed my abilities reflected on our system of government. After the Worlds, the media wrote that I was done and over the hill. I chose not to listen to them. It would have been a waste of time. Listening to negative feedback does nothing for anyone. There are so many people in the world ready to find fault. I don't believe in giving them power by paying attention to them. I believe in being your own biggest supporter because that means you will always have someone in your corner.

I returned to Deva. Undaunted by my experiences at the Worlds, I continued to train. My relationship with Bela began to change. He started to treat me as an adult, to consult me on my own training and ideas. There were days when I disagreed with the number of repetitions of skills necessary; for example, Bela would tell me to do five dismounts from the beam, and I knew I only needed to do three. He started trusting me to know what my body needed. He knew I wasn't being lazy, that I was being smart. He also began to let me teach some of the little ones their compulsory routines. I loved coaching. I was demanding but understanding. If the gymnasts were too tired to finish their last repetition, I'd say, "Okay, but you do two for me tomorrow," and they always would. They came to me for counsel, and I really liked taking care of them and being helpful.

My routine workouts changed. When I was younger, I had to learn skills and do countless repetitions because I needed to store lots of knowledge in my bag so I would have things to pull out and use during competitions. By 1979, all my skills were automatic. Whatever I needed was already in my bag, and so I just had to keep my body in shape. I did far fewer repetitions of strengthening skills such as sit-ups and only three hours of training, which included running; refining dance skills; practicing small sequences of my bar, beam, and floor exercises; and stretching. I spent about eighteen minutes a day of actual time on the apparatus plus conditioning. Think about it, a routine on the bars is only thirty-five seconds long, and then there's a ten-minute recuperation. The same goes for each event. Changing my equipment and shoes cost a little bit of time. Plus, there's warm-up and cool-down time.

Whatever I did worked. Seven months after the Worlds, I won the all-around gold at the European Championships. I was tall, lean, and unbelievably powerful. I was a new Nadia—transformed. Being a champion is about pushing yourself beyond the possible and believing in your abilities even when everyone around you says you aren't capable. Over the hill? I wasn't even close. I was back on top, and the only way I'd step down again was by my own volition.

What did you mean, my friend, when you wrote that in return for accomplishing my goals, I sacrificed my childhood? Just when I think you're starting to understand me! Never have I thought about gymnastics as a sacrifice. Never. You have been misled by the stories you've read in books, magazines, and newspapers about how emotionally devastating gymnastics can be and about the supposedly destructive relationships between young girls and their coaches, food, and pain. I am not saying that some gymnasts have not suffered. I do not know them and therefore can't judge. And I am also not saying that all coaches are good or that many young girls don't face eating disorders or lapses in judgment in relation to dealing with physical problems and pain. I'm just saying that I never had those experiences.

Gymnastics was never a torture for me. Even as a child, I knew that everyone did something for a living. You can sacrifice your time to travel to a job or spend countless hours at a desk . . . for what? Maybe it's to make a better jingle for a laundry detergent. Maybe you'll choose to stand on a factory line and build a car, or perhaps you'll sell real estate. Why is that better or worse than what I chose? Life is full of sacrifices, but I loved what I was doing, which is more than can be said for most people. Do you love your life? If so, why are you seeking answers from others? Your letters are not just filled with questions about tabloid fodder, they are deep and real and probing because you are searching for something more in your own life. I don't know if I have any answers for you, but I'm willing to share my experiences.

I thrived at the gym, where it smelled like mats and chalk and felt like a home away from home. There was no child abuse in my life. As children at the experimental school in Onesti, we had everything done for us. Our rooms were warm and always cleaned, there was more than enough food, and the cooking and dishes were always done for us. The only thing we had to do was gymnastics, and no one forced us. Meanwhile, people in Romania were literally starving at the time. Maybe that's why I find the idea that I sacrificed my childhood so bizarre. For gymnasts in Communist countries, the sport gave us more than it could ever take away. Yes, there were tragic accidents, but considering what we were doing, it's actually impressive there were so few.

What did I miss, then? Going to the mall and hanging out? Dating boys before I was emotionally ready for a relationship? Video games? We didn't have those! I didn't even know what a VCR was. In Onesti, all there was to do was walk around the village. I was a gymnast for such a small period of time, yet it gave me so much. What does a kid really do between the age of six and sixteen that's so valuable? Today, I'd be a forty-something nobody if I hadn't been a gymnast. Even if I hadn't become number one in my field, I'd still be more than I would have been without goals and accomplishments. I've done something with my life and learned about strength, determination, and drive.

You may think that it's easy for me to write this because I succeeded in my sport, but there were years when I did not succeed. Life wasn't handed to me on a plate of gold. Nothing fell into my lap. I went for things, and sometimes I got them and sometimes I didn't. Hard work will always get you somewhere. If you have a little talent and work very hard, then you have a shot at being a big winner. And if you have a lucky star in your hand, then you may just accomplish your goals. Above all else, you have to be hungry to do something unbelievable.

I've read that Bela once said about gymnasts, "These girls are like little scorpions. You put them all in a bottle, and one scorpion will come out alive. That scorpion will be champion." I was always a survivor, and perhaps that eventually made me a champion. Regardless, gymnastics gave me a sense of myself and made me stronger, both mentally and physically. *Devastated* is a word I don't even know. Everything in life can be fixed somehow.

Don't you see that for me, *sacrifice* and *gymnastics* are not synonymous. The concepts exist at two different poles on two different planets in two different universes. I look at gymnasts today and think they have it much better than I did. Maybe that's just about being an adult and looking at children. But for one, the equipment is much safer. Our beam was made of wood, and now it's a softer and more forgiving material. The floors are much springier, so gymnasts can go higher and do skills with more safety. I wish I'd had a chance to play on those when I was ten years old. And young gymnasts have so many more options in their lives these days.

Kids today are also savvier than we were back then. There are computers and television and a host of other educational and sports-related opportunities. But no child, no matter where he is born, sacrifices time if he doesn't like what he's doing. Sure, there are some disturbed parents and children out there, and for them, I'm sorry that any given sport is unhealthy. And there have always been bad coaches, though today, it's simple to research their backgrounds and make an educated decision about who is best for your child.

You've asked, "What of the pressure?" Well, again, I have only my own opinion. Mostly, it's people in the United States who contend that young athletes experience too much pressure. Personally, I don't think that children have any pressure. Adults have pressure, but what does a kid know about it except what she puts on her own shoulders? Maybe it's different now. When I was young, at least before the 1976 Olympics, no one expected anything from me. There was no media pressure. There was nothing to lose. What was my mother going to do—put me out on the street if I didn't succeed as a gymnast?

My mother never got involved with my sport. That is not the case with everyone. Sometimes I see parents getting too involved. They should be doing their own thing, while still supporting their kids' efforts. Too much involvement changes a child's perceptions of what he is doing and why. Goals get clouded, on both the adult and the child's sides. That's when problems occur. To the parents, I say that in the United States, there are approximately 4 million kids doing some level of gymnastics, and only *six* of them will actually make it to the Olympics. Those are steep odds, to say the least.

In the United States, there are so many gymnastics programs, many of them free, that any child can see if she enjoys the sport. From that point on, a level of personal and financial commitment will grow if it's meant to be. In Romania, you had to move away from your family, live in a sports complex, and train with a specific coach to succeed. In the United States, there are a lot of good coaches, and though some children and their families move as a result of their dedication to gymnastics, it doesn't have to be that way. I don't know if that's better or worse, just different.

You want to know what I think? Let a child have the chance to find out what sport she loves and to see what she's good at. If she doesn't like it, fine, let her do something else. But keep her active because it's good for her body and mind. Kids shouldn't be obligated to do a sport just because they show promise. No matter how much a parent wants it, the child has to want it more.

Of course, it may be possible for a talented child to eventually win Olympic medals, but most kids change their minds about what they want to do within weeks, months, or a few years. Even if they don't, so few young gymnasts are actually good at all four events, and to be a successful elite gymnast, you have to be great at each and astoundingly consistent. So you can bet that most kids just aren't going to make it, and that's okay. What's important is to develop a healthy sense of self-esteem.

You want to know what I'd do if a child came to me at age seven and told me that she was going to shoot for the moon? I would never say that she's lost her mind. Things are possible, and I'd never clip somebody's wings. Yes, you can do that, I'd say, but it's going to be very hard. I'm here to help because I know what happens when you miss a skill like a back handspring on the beam and get frustrated or have fear. I've been in your shoes. To her parents, I might say that the moon is far away and very high and that it can be a lonely place. I'd say to be careful of letting their child attempt to visit the moon unless they are ready to catch her if she falls and to deal with the consequences. Not every child is meant to be a Nadia. Sometimes I am amazed that I never got broken.

As a result of my experiences and those of my husband, Bart Conner, the gymnasium and programs we run at the Bart Conner Gymnastics Academy in Norman, Oklahoma, aren't designed only for those elite gymnasts who want to go to the Olympics. We love to coach and watch kids—both the gifted ones and those just enjoying themselves—learn new skills and gain strength and self-confidence. Our biggest focus is on getting our gymnasts scholarships to good colleges. We like the idea that we make the sport more accessible and help kids who couldn't pay for an education to get one through their athletic talents.

But back to your question, my friend, about the physical toll of gymnastics. I never blame a sport for things that happen in life. There are accidents, but I believe they only happen when a gymnast is either incredibly unlucky or unprepared. Of course, there is always a physical price to pay in my sport. I have pains here and there from my time as a gymnast. It's pretty normal wear and tear, considering what I was doing with my body. I made decisions for myself back then. In a world where everything is bad for you in excess, I chose to listen to my body and take care of it. There was only one time, in Fort Worth, Texas, when I ignored my body's pain signals.

I'm not naive. Just like you, I've read that U.S. gymnast Betty Okino refused to stop training when she was diagnosed with a stress fracture in her right elbow. Eventually, her arm broke. She also ripped the tendon from the bone below her knee while running toward a vault and had stress fractures in her back and ultimately shattered several vertebrae. Okino, like countless other elite gymnasts, was willing to risk her health to be in the Olympics. Kelly Garrison had more than twenty stress fractures in her back from years of competitions, and Brandy Johnson, one of the top U.S. gymnasts, competed at the 1989 Worlds with a fractured foot. I don't know any of their personal reasons or if adults in their lives should have stopped them. I refuse to be anyone's judge.

All elite athletes deal with pain. Some of their bodies are unable to handle the intense training. I have been through the pain of conditioning, but while I was competing, I never suffered torn tendons, broken bones, or shattered vertebrae. If I had, I don't know what I would have done. It's hard to balance intense desire with injuries and to know whether the threat of disappointment would have overshadowed common sense. Some gymnasts pop ibuprofen every day. Others are willing to numb the pain of fractures with injections before competitions and deal with the consequences later. Is it right? No. Did I do it to a lesser extent during my career? Yes. Did anyone force me? No way. But then, I was a kid, and some would point out that I didn't know any better.

And what about the emotional toll? You wrote me that you've read about the devastation some gymnasts experience when they don't accomplish their goals. I can sympathize but not empathize with them because that is not what happened to me. I had tough times, but I always fought my way back to the top, and what I came to understand through that process was priceless. Gymnastics is a difficult sport, but life is tougher. What I learned about ignoring my detractors, focusing on my goals, and overcoming seemingly impossible challenges during my gymnastics career has helped me. I don't know if I could have left my family, risked my life by defecting from my homeland, or found a new life in a foreign country if I had not struggled to overcome challenges in the past. What you learn as a child and teen and the life skills that come out of difficult situations are vital tools for adulthood. It doesn't matter whether you win gold medals. What matters is that you strive to be your best and then struggle to be even better.

You want to know about the darkness in a sport that was always filled with light for me. I can't answer your questions about anorexia and gymnastics because though I can sympathize with gymnasts who experience eating disorders, once again I can't relate. First, in Romania, most gymnasts considered themselves lucky to get three good meals a day. Second, we weren't in charge of our diets. The team doctor decided all of our meals, and we simply ate them because we didn't know there was any other choice. Third, there were no trips to the candy store (we didn't have a candy store, and even if we had, we didn't have much money for sweets) or late-night bingeing on food at sleepovers. Of course, like any kids, we did try to sneak candy and other sweets we were given by friends into the dorm, and we succeeded sometimes. But our movements were quite controlled, and there was no way we could gain weight with the amount of exercise we did.

The truth is that if we had gained too much weight, we would not have been great gymnasts and could have gotten hurt. Only by balancing calories can any gymnast maintain her weight and delay puberty. Puberty can end a girl's career, and overweight gymnasts, no matter how talented, can't be as powerful or graceful as competitors who maintain a healthier body weight. This is just a fact. My friend, it might seem unfair, but a soccer player needs power and muscles; a football player must be fast, strong, and sometimes heavier than he desires; a skater needs graceful lines; and gymnasts must be light and lean.

As a result of eating well and being under the guidance of a physician, I was given the gift of a strong body and bones, though my mother of course attributes these things to a different source. She loves to remind me that *she* is most responsible for my health, saying that when I was born, I took everything good out of her body. I understand that there are real consequences for young gymnasts who do not eat a healthy, well-balanced diet. I urge parents to look at their child's psyche, body type, and nutritional needs when helping that child decide if a career in gymnastics is the right choice for his or her physical *and* emotional well-being.

I have tried to answer your questions about the emotional and physical tolls of gymnastics from my own perspective. I have written about overcoming challenges and winning the gold at the European Championships just five months after my poor showing at the 1978 Worlds. Although I've expressed how gymnastics has affected my life in countless positive ways, you are understandably still very curious about the one time I mentioned when I did ignore my body's pain signals. Before I tell you what really happened in Fort Worth, let me say that though I pushed the envelope that day, I believe I was never in danger of serious injury. One of the reasons my gymnastics career was so long and successful was because of the common sense I exhibited.

After the Worlds and the European Championships, I spent the next few months training and competing, with success after success. I had achieved a higher level of fitness than ever before and believed my results at the World Championships in Fort Worth would be no different. But there were problems before our team ever arrived in Texas. The Romanian government sent us to Mexico a month before the Worlds to train in a gymnasium on U.S. apparatus they'd purchased, to make certain we would be comfortable going into the competition. The differences in the equipment were very small, but even tiny things such as the feel of the floor material and the measurement systems of the vault and bars can throw off a gymnast when the pressure is on. They also wanted us to get used to the heat and humidity, since the climate in Mexico was similar to that in Texas. But instead of getting prepared, we got a vicious stomach flu. Suffering from diarrhea and nausea, it was difficult to train. I lost almost 10 pounds and was incredibly weak.

I didn't like being far away from home for so long. I wrote letters to my mom, telling her I was homesick and disliked the spicy food. Plus, the new generation of gymnasts on my team was coming up, and it was time for me to move on. While traveling, I had to live under the rules Bela imposed on the younger gymnasts even though I was eighteen years old. I obeyed him but didn't like the restrictions. Once again, we began to have small disagreements.

The entire team looked gaunt and pale when we arrived in Texas. The Western media immediately wrote that we were no longer the energetic, cute little girls of the past; we looked starved and unhappy. Unfortunately, they never bothered to ask our coaches why we appeared so sickly. At the time, none of us realized that the media were talking about us or that people were focused on the way we looked. I forced myself through the compulsories—I was the team leader, and the younger gymnasts depended on me to set an example. If I could do it, they could, too. Going into the optionals, we were five-tenths of a point behind the Russians. Despite our poor health, we had a chance to win the team gold, but I had an additional problem I'd been ignoring that was going to threaten our chances and my own ability to compete.

I had scratched myself with the buckle of my hand guards during practice toward the end of our stay in Mexico, and I think that chalk, friction, sweat, and dirt caused an infection. A small, red bump began to form. It grew bigger and bigger and started to get inflamed. I thought I should massage it—which only made it worse. It became more and more difficult to bend my arm. By the time I entered the arena for the optional portion of the competition, my wrist was red and very swollen, and I was in considerable pain.

When Bela saw my injury, he instructed me to see what I could do on each apparatus during the warm-up period. I tried to do my bar routine, but my wrist was too swollen, and I had no range of motion or strength. Bela told me to just touch each apparatus when I was called for every event so that I could remain in the competition. (If I didn't present myself to the judges and touch the equipment, I would have been disqualified.) When the rest of the team saw my inability to perform, they fell apart. They'd lost their leader, and all of their inexperience and fears overwhelmed them. But a huge smile lit Bela's face, and he gave one of his famous pep talks.

"You can win the floor, beam, bars, and vault. You can win the individual all-around as well as the team all-around title. Go for it, dammit! If you want to prove that you've been working hard, preparing hard, then go out there and eat them up. Are you afraid of those suckers! . . . I guarantee you that nobody, nobody worked harder for this competition than you have. . . . Do your best. Can we do it?!"

The team was fired up. And it is a fact that their scores were high and that they were poised to beat the Russians. At the start of every event, I presented myself to the judges and touched each apparatus, then sat back down. My compulsory scores from the previous day (which were carried over to the optionals and added to the gymnast's total score) were so high that had I performed, I could have fallen a couple of times and probably still won. But there was no need for me to compete until the beam, when one of our gymnasts fell. Suddenly, my score was necessary for the win.

Bela recalls turning to me and asking, "Nadia, did you ever think that you had any obligations to your team members? I have to tell you that you do have obligations, 'cause all of these little guys carried all the hard parts of your victories. These are the ones who built your scores for so many years. These are the ones who have never been recognized for that. These are the silent soldiers who carried the hard part of your glory. . . . Did you ever think that you owed me or Marta anything for what has happened over the years? If you truly feel that for all our work and consideration you owe us something, then walk up right now and do a beautiful thing . . . do your beam routine."

Of that moment when I talked to Bela before attempting my beam routine, I only vaguely remember him asking me after my teammate fell if I could compete. Of course I said yes because Bela believed I could and because the team needed me to perform. I told Bela that I couldn't do the mount, since it required pressure on both my hands, but that I would make up a different mount. My friend, even if I fell, I might still have had a chance to push the team over the top. I didn't need a pep talk or any convincing; I would have supported my teammates no matter what. We always helped each other like sisters, and if it was possible for me to perform without killing myself, I'd try. After so many years, I had a bit of knowledge stored up about how much I could do.

Looking back, I know that my beam performance was not really a sacrifice for my team or my coach. The routine wasn't painful if I didn't bend my arm. And because I was using my right hand most of the time, I could avoid some pain on my left by putting most of the pressure on my right hand during skills such as back handsprings. I had no fear because I wasn't sure what was going to happen, so consequently, I didn't make any mistakes.

Today, Bela says that he never believed it was truly possible for me to perform well that day. Despite the fact that the beam was a leg event and that I could do one-handed handstands and handsprings, he didn't think I'd be capable of performing. But it is a fact that I did perform that day on the beam. I used three fingers from my damaged hand to balance through skills, and though I felt some pain, concentration blotted out most of it. I never fell, and I stuck my dismount. My score was 9.95, and my team returned to first place. I couldn't compete in the rest of the events, but we still won the all-around team title.

I do not believe that I risked permanent damage to my arm that day. I do not believe that Bela would ever have put me in that position. But I do believe that my sense of team obligation and my desire to fulfill my coach's expectation had something to do with my decision to perform. I wonder, today, if it was even a decision back then, or if I just followed Bela's orders because that is what I always did. It's impossible to know.

So, I guess there's the answer to your question, friend. I don't believe I ever sacrificed my health for a single competition. There was nothing heroic about my efforts that day. No pain, no gain. Sounds simple and trite, but it's true. If an athlete doesn't have some pain, it means she hasn't worked hard enough. At the Worlds, I made informed decisions based on my own knowledge and a level of trust in those around me.

That night after the optionals, I went to the hospital and had surgery on my wrist. The doctors gave me a general anesthetic and cleaned out the infection, which had traveled up my arm in red lines. I remained in the hospital for a day and then left with a drain still implanted in my arm because the doctors didn't think the cut was ready to be completely closed. I flew home with the team, and a group of doctors was waiting when I arrived in Bucharest. They wanted to take me to the hospital, but I insisted on returning to my home in Deva. A nurse accompanied me, and when my wound had drained completely, she stitched me up.

Today, I have a two-inch scar from the Worlds. I also have the knowledge that I faced adversity and thrived. I could easily have refused to compete, but I'm not that kind of person. If I say I can't do something, I'm lying and cheating myself of the results of my efforts. Some people say that it's because of all the extra efforts I made as a child that I became better than everyone else. Don't be fooled, though, I have always looked out for myself.

Here is a little secret, friend. Throughout my years of training and competition, I always kept a reserve of energy. Let's say that I knew that I could do fifteen laps of the stadium. I'd tell Bela I could do ten and give myself some reserve, some padding. Even if he'd say that I should do twelve, that meant I was capable of doing three more. I worked out in pain, but I knew the difference between pain that was tolerable and pain that didn't help me and lessened my abilities. I followed my instincts, as I always have, and they led me to safety. You seem to want me to tell you what is unhealthy or too much for other gymnasts. I cannot answer that question. Bela pushed me hard, but the reason he could never break me is because he never truly knew my limits.

Courage?

The Romanian team's conditioning exercises for the uneven bars were intense. Every day, we did three sets of five glide kip casts to handstands, which require the gymnasts to support their entire bodies on the bars with their arms by leaning their shoulders forward and kicking their heels backward into a handstand. We also did three sets of ten V-ups, which are like sit-ups except the gymnast hangs from the high bar and pikes her feet to her face.

In addition to conditioning exercises, we worked on dozens of different sequences from our bar routines each day. We'd do three tricks in a row or start near the end of a routine and do the final elements and then our dismounts. Plus, we'd do five complete exercises each day, two in the morning and three in the afternoon. Our entire time on the bars was one hour and fifteen minutes per day. Working on the uneven bars is extremely strenuous, and spending any more time than this would have been too much for our bodies to handle.

When I returned to Deva after the 1979 World Championships in Texas, I was confused. I was too old to continue traveling with the young gymnasts on my team and to live under Bela and Marta's rule. I could no longer be a marionette and let others pull my strings. I wanted to be in control. But control is an illusion, especially in a Communist country. That was one of the lessons that I had to learn again and again, until I finally listened to what God (or whatever higher power you choose to believe in) was saying to me. It happens a lot in life—you get whispered to, tapped on the shoulder, knocked over the head, maybe even flattened by a car . . . until you finally hear what you were supposed to have learned long ago and then make a change.

Back in Deva, I continued to live with my mother. She had a good friend who became a sort of mentor to me. He asked me upon my return if I had given more thought to going to a university. I said no, and he replied that if I wanted to do more with my life, I needed an education. People with diplomas were hired first, and gold medals wouldn't get me a job. What university? I asked him. He suggested the Polytechnic Institute in Bucharest, where you could receive a college degree in sports education as well as a host of other sports-related fields. I was nineteen and decided to push through one more year of gymnastics and then apply to the university. I wanted to compete in the 1980 Olympic Games, but I was done with living and training in Deva. Bela and Marta gave me their blessings, and I returned to Bucharest.

As you'll learn soon enough, nothing comes without a price. I trained hard in Bucharest, but I was also fighting a problem with sciatica and had pain down my leg.

Sometimes I couldn't feel one of my toes because the nerve was being pinched. I did a lot of physical therapy and slept on a hard surface. Instead of forcing anything, I did the minimum necessary to get by and be able to compete. Mostly, the pain bothered me when I was sitting, not training. But I stayed away from any specific gymnastic skills that would make it worse.

Most gymnasts have trouble with their backs, but after that bout with sciatica, I never did again, though I don't know why. As I said, I survived gymnastics with almost no repercussions. It wasn't until 1994, during an exhibition gymnastics show in Wyoming, that I was finally injured. Earlier that day, I'd learned that Monica Seles had been stabbed on a tennis court in Germany. I was upset and had been thinking about her all day. During my exhibition routine, I was doing a double twist on the floor and lost my concentration. I should have been thinking about my performance and, at that moment, my landing, not Monica. I felt something snap and heat in my knee. With a sense of shock, I motioned for help.

What a strange sensation that was; the gymnasium was a world where I had total control . . . up until that moment. Funny how we are misled into thinking we have any control at all. For me, it was so easy to think of myself as invincible. I had never broken a bone, and I was certain that's what I'd done in Wyoming because I had no reference point for the pain. I'm going to have some kind of surgery, I thought as I was helped off the mat. My instincts were still intact. And I did wind up having knee surgery. It was a success.

I would like to say a bit about my mother here because she, too, has always had great instincts. It was my mother who insisted on saving all the money I made during my gymnastics career, whereas I, like any kid, would have spent it. When I moved to Bucharest in 1979, my mother and brother again came with me. We needed a place to live and heard that there was a lady who wanted to leave the country because her husband had defected and she planned to join him. We bought her house. We could never have afforded even a quarter of the cost without the funds my mother had saved up from the monetary awards I'd received in competitions. The government, over the years, had retained a percentage of money from my salary to pay for my room and board, and by combining our savings and that money, we were able to make a down payment on the house. I figured by the time I was sixty years old, I might actually own it free and clear.

My "salary" in Romania equaled about US $100 a month. I couldn't afford to pay for the heat in the house, so my mother got a job as a cashier at a local store. The house was still too large to heat in its entirety (it had three bedrooms), so my mother, brother, and I lived and slept in the kitchen during the winter. Meanwhile, the government continued to retain a percentage of my salary to make monthly mortgage payments on our home.

As I've told you, one of the biggest misperceptions about my life in Romania is that I was living like royalty. The truth is that when I moved from Deva back to Bucharest, I did not even want to have any friends because I didn't want them to know just how poor I was. I didn't want them to see that I didn't have all that they might have imagined. I was ashamed because I was an Olympic champion training for the next Games and people expected me to have everything.

As a young adult, it's hard to negotiate between people's expectations of you versus your own expectations and the reality of your situation. It's impossible not to feel upset when what you believe you deserve doesn't mesh with reality. It's impossible not to feel upset when other people believe you are living a life that is not, in truth, your own. Figuring out how to find dignity and happiness within yourself, instead of searching for it from other people or from material things, is one of life's toughest lessons. It took me many years to learn that lesson, but with it came peace.

Friend, back in Romania I didn't have many material things. I had a car that my mother had bought with some of our savings, but it was little more than a tin can with four wheels, not a Mercedes. Sure, there were some Romanian athletes who made money, such as soccer players, who, for whatever reason, were considered huge national heroes and deserving of monetary rewards for their accomplishments. But in gymnastics, there was very little money to be made, and I was given only a small amount from my exhibition tours. I don't know who in the government decided on the amount of money and special treatment that went to individual athletes, but whoever it was didn't think much of gymnasts, even though the Romanian people considered me to be a national hero.

Back then, Olympic athletes in Communist countries had no opportunities to make money off endorsements or public-speaking engagements. We didn't have sport agents, and our only "representation" came from our government. So if the government didn't see fit to give us much money, then we didn't have much money. Today, top athletes have so many opportunities for fame and wealth, and I don't know if that helps or hurts their careers. Gymnastics was never about money for me, but it was humiliating to have worked so hard, in part for the glory of my country, and to still be struggling to survive.

In Bucharest, I continued to train, but I was mentally finished with gymnastics, this time for real. I played around a lot in the gym, but I maintained my level of fitness. When Bela came for a visit, he was amazed at my abilities and said I would definitely be on the Romanian team. The Romanian government touted the 1980 Olympics as the first all-Communist Games because the United States and other democratic countries were boycotting as a result of the Russians' invasion of Afghanistan (several non-Communist countries did participate, however). The boycott didn't make much difference to me. I'm not judging whether it was warranted. Back then, I paid no attention to politics. The bottom line for me was that our gymnastics team was competing against the Russians and Germans because they were our strongest competitors. American gymnast weren't on our level at that time, so they wouldn't be missed at the Games.

You mentioned something in your last letter about how courageous I was to compete in the 1980 Olympics. I must admit I'm a little confused. Do you think it took courage to compete because I was older than the rest of the team? It didn't, since the truth is that I was better. I knew at the time that the competition going into Moscow would be tough, but when wasn't it tough? I believe that everyone reaps what he or she has sown. I was a great gymnast and deserved to compete at the 1980 Games and to do well.

In Moscow, we walked into the mouth of a lion's den; it was the Russians' home turf, but the only fear I felt entering the arena was the nerves that come before the start of any competition. The hardest time is always the waiting. The waiting kills me and twists my stomach into knots. But once the competition begins, the fear is gone. There's nothing to do about nerves except to stay focused and know that the feeling will go away once it is replaced by concentration. If a gymnast can't replace fear with concentration during a competition, then she will have more problems than a few knots in her stomach.

Did you know that we had team psychologists who trained us to do routines over and over again in our heads? I could perform every movement, leap, twist, and somersault and almost feel each apparatus beneath my hands just by closing my eyes and summoning up the events. Those same psychologists also taught us to see our capacity to solve problems by working on actual puzzles, brainteasers with pieces we needed to unlock, and cubes with colors that had to be manipulated in patterns. They tested how quickly we became frustrated by those puzzles and helped us to work on managing our frustration levels. We did a lot of that type of training. Bela used to bring people from the street into our training sessions to make noise and try to break our focus by yelling and whistling. Sometimes we even practiced doing our routines without warming up just in case such a situation ever arose. If they'd awakened me at 3:00 A.M., I could have done a perfect beam routine. We were prepared for everything, and a little booing couldn't hurt us.

Day one of the Olympics, Bela patted all of us on the backs and told us we could do it; he told us we'd do great. But as it happened, I didn't do that great. I fell during my bar routine. It happened so fast that there was nothing I could do to save my performance. One minute

I was up there, the next I was on the mat. As a gymnast, you naturally hope it doesn't happen, but it does. And there's no way to go back and fix it. That happens in life, too, those times you wish you could just do something over so that the results would be better. The only thing to do is try again and try harder. Overwhelm the negative. After my fall on the bars, I've heard that many of my fellow Romanians wanted to blame the Russians or the flashes of cameras for my mistake. Neither had anything to do with it. I just lost my concentration and fell.

You might not believe this, but it does not take that much courage to get back on any apparatus after a fall. It's actually easy. Once a mistake is made, nothing worse can really happen. It's a done deal. The worst part about a mistake is dealing with the disappointment once the routine is over.

You've asked me if after a mistake, I ever hoped another gymnast would fall. The fact is, I rarely watched my competitors during competitions because I was usually warming up or performing at the same time. If not, I was helping to move the springboard or doing measurements for the teammate who competed after I was done with an event. Almost every moment during a competition is planned out—there's no time for idle thoughts. There's certainly no time to wish anyone difficulties.

I rarely watched my own teammates perform at events for two reasons. First, Bela suggested that it would help all of us concentrate if we didn't watch each other because that was just another distraction. Second, if one of our gymnasts messed up, it put too much pressure on me. Only one person on a team is allowed to make a mistake on any event because the lowest score is thrown out. If there had already been a mistake before I competed, then I had to hit an event with no reserve. That was too much pressure. And if I made the mistake? I never spent time trying to calculate what needed to happen for me to win. That was a waste of time. So was competing against my teammates. If a fellow gymnast does well, then the whole team benefits.

People tend to believe that it's a catfight between the gymnasts. What they don't understand is that everyone knows what their teammates are capable of doing in any event. It's not like you need to spy on them. Gymnasts accomplish the skills they perform in training. You cannot do more in a competition than you can in training. It's not possible. Maybe you stick a landing here or there and that's better, but there are no big surprises. Gymnasts compete against themselves. Nobody else really makes a difference in the big picture. But the media like to play up rivalries and create heroes.

Our team as a whole performed so well in the team competition at the 1980 Olympics that we were second to the Russians. Despite my earlier fall off the bars, I still had the chance to win the gold in the individual all-around finals, but I didn't assume I would. Another gymnast who'd done all four events without any errors could potentially knock me out of first place because my low score from the earlier round when I fell off the bars was carried over into the final competition. That meant I had to perform a near perfect routine on each apparatus, plus another gymnast had to make a mistake so that my score would be higher than hers.

Today, the rules are different. Gymnasts' scores don't carry over into a final competition. So, if you fall off the beam during the team competition, you aren't penalized during the individual all-around. It's a good change

because it makes a competition more interesting and because each girl has the chance to win: One bad day or a
single mistake can't ruin an entire Olympics. But in
1980, we were still using the old rules, and though I
wanted to win the individual all-around, I didn't think
I had much of a chance.

The beam was my final event at the 1980 Games. Yelena Davydova was set to finish on the bars, and if she
made no mistakes, she would take the all-around gold. In
the competition order, I was to perform second on the
beam, and Yelena would be the sixth and final gymnast on
the bars. Simple, right? Wrong. After the first competitor
finished her beam routine, I prepared for the judges to
signal my turn. But they didn't. Instead, they huddled together, and I thought they were conferring about a score.
Meanwhile, the bar routines continued. First, second,
third . . . I still waited for my turn on the beam.

Bela instructed me to do some more warm-ups on
the floor. As I said, the waiting was the hardest part. The
fourth and fifth girls did their bar routines. Impatient,
Bela tried to ask the judges what the holdup was, but
they had no answer. Yelena did her bar routine—and
there were no major mistakes. She received a 9.95. I was
finally motioned to the beam. Apart from a slight bob-
ble, I turned in a very solid routine and was scored a
9.85. That was a good number in Moscow; if we'd been
in Romania, I probably would have gotten a higher
score. Home turf makes quite a difference. No one can
argue with a perfect routine, but if there's the slightest
mistake and a gymnast is competing in another country
. . . well, the scores just won't be as high.

Davydova won the gold. I wasn't that disappointed.
I'd won the silver. But Bela was angry because he

thought I'd deserved a 9.95 on the beam. More than that, he believed that the judges had conspired to have Davydova perform her bar routine before I competed on the beam so that they could score her higher and ensure her the gold medal. Personally, I don't believe that's true, but I can't know for certain. At the time, I just sat on a mat and watched Bela run around the arena demanding to see individual scores and yelling for justice.

I knew that the Romanian people were watching the Games on television and that they would be upset because they would believe we'd been cheated. But nothing at the 1980 Olympics was different from past competitions. For me, I knew I had made a mistake on the bars. That day, Yelena just performed better. I didn't think about scoring or whether the judges were playing fair. I'd made a mistake; losing the gold was my fault alone. And still, I'd moved from fourth to second, and that was satisfying in its own right.

I have heard that Bela got into a lot of trouble when he returned to Romania for disrupting the Moscow Olympics by making a scene about the fairness of the judges' scores. A friend told me that the people were filled with hate for the Russians and believed that we were cheated. *But I went down on the bars*, I thought, *did no one see that?* It's a strange feeling when what you know for certain clashes with what the media or the people of your country are saying. I was baffled about the situation, but in my heart, I knew what had happened and refused to lie to myself or anyone else. If you are not true to yourself, then your life becomes a lie. I was told that Bela was called to Bucharest to report to the Central Committee, composed of the powerful leaders under Ceausescu who ran the country.

It has been said that Ceausescu never liked Bela because he was of Hungarian heritage and that the president was looking for an excuse to bring him trouble. Lt. Gen. Ion Mihai Pacepa, the former head of Romanian Intelligence (he was the highest-ranking defector from the Eastern bloc) wrote in his exposé, *Red Horizons*, that Ceausescu was a fanatical nationalist. "Only ethnic Romanians going back two generations and born within the Romanian borders are allowed to hold Party and government positions affecting national security," Pacepa said in his book. "For the job I held in the DIE [Departamentul de Informatii Externe—the Foreign Intelligence Service], the requirement was pure Romanian blood going back three generations."

I cannot say that I was surprised by the time I read Pacepa's book about Ceausescu's nature. But I'm constantly surprised to read that Ceausescu really cared that much about the Karolyis or me. Pacepa said that "by the end of 1977 Ceausescu had decided to change Nadia's coaches. 'I don't want to share Nadia's fame with a couple of dirty boanghen [a derogatory term for Hungarians],' he said. 'We have to find Romanian coaches for her, people of Romanian blood.'" That was the time when the government decided that Bela and I should have a trial separation and I was moved to Bucharest. It's strange to interpret your own history through the eyes of someone else. I like to believe that I *chose* to go to Bucharest, but I'm not so naive that I can't accept other possibilities.

Regardless of what was said between Ceausescu and his most trusted adviser, Bela recalls that when he arrived at the committee headquarters in 1980, he was forced to stand before a table of men and explain why he had disturbed the Games, spoken to the Western media (Bela told an ABC affiliate reporter that the Games were corrupt), and insulted our "Soviet friends." He was told that he'd humiliated Romania and Ceausescu, and his life was threatened; the possibility of imprisonment for his "crimes" was also raised. I was not there, but I can say that Romanians have gone to prison for lesser offenses.

Meanwhile, I went with the flow and didn't talk to anyone about the Games or make any comments. I was settling down to life in Bucharest.

The Struggle

In Romania, the process of creating our floor routines began with Geza Pozsar, our choreographer. Geza would play different kinds of music and have all the gymnasts out on the floor dancing. He'd watch us and see what type of music we moved to best. Then he'd have each girl try to create specific moves to go with the music so that he could envision what kind of choreography would work for each of us. I loved to dance to Harry Belafonte, so Geza used that music for me.

Back when I was competing, there were no tapes or compact discs for music, and each gymnast executed her floor routine in competitions to a song performed live by a piano player. Only one accompanying instrument was allowed. That might seem simple compared to today's floor routine music, but there were advantages. A compact disc won't wait for a gymnast to recover from a mistake, but a piano player will.

Life in Bucharest after the 1980 Olympics was, at best, mundane. I was going to school, supporting my brother, who was living with me and also at school, and trying to survive through the second half of each month because I was so broke. I'm not proud of this, but you should know the truth, my friend: My situation bothered me a lot. If I'd always lived my life as a "regular" person, I never would have known any different. But I'd won numerous international competitions and made my country proud, and I still had nothing.

Life isn't fair, I knew that . . . but in addition, it was exhausting. An acquaintance used to get me clothes because she worked in a clothing factory; I'd trade fruits and vegetables every day so that I could figure out what to make for dinner each night. To this day, I don't have recipes for anything, I just improvise with what's available. I'm a good cook, very inventive. If a friend had a little extra fish, I'd trade it for a piece of cheese. It was a constant challenge. I was twenty and felt the weight of my life as well as my family's, and at times it was overwhelming.

The only "special" groceries I received were two loaves of bread from a friend who worked in the bread factory. This was a favor but not a government favor. Getting food was extremely difficult for everybody. We had an old neighbor, Aleca Petre, who must have been seventy, and he used to wake up at 4:00 A.M. and stand in line at the grocery store in the freezing winter weather, waiting to see if there was anything on the shelves. Usually, there was only mayonnaise, mustard, and beans. That was it. He'd bring us a few bottles of milk and on rare occasions a piece of meat. I'd always invite him to join us for meals, even though we didn't have much. That is the way Romanians are: We share what we have.

Not a day went by that we didn't share something with our neighbors. We used to joke that we'd borrow each other's old meat bones to make soup. It was a tragic and difficult life for everyone. People would have been happy if they could just have put something on the table for their kids to eat. Meanwhile, all of the good food in our country was being exported. I later came to understand from newspaper articles and books that it was Ceausescu's way of filling his coffers and paying off the debt he'd incurred on behalf of our country (I'll tell you more about that later, if you are interested). I realized when I left gymnastics just how lucky I had been. When I was training, I ate incredibly well by comparison. It's no wonder I still find it difficult to complain about those days, as I was so much better off than most everyone else. But when my gymnastics days were over, I was left in the same unhappy position as the rest of the people of my country.

Life was unfair and difficult, but I still considered myself to be lucky because I had the opportunity to attend school. That meant I could get a job outside of the factories. The sports diploma at the university was a four-year program, but students didn't have to attend lectures; instead, they took books and assignments home and then took exams with the rest of the student body at the end of each course. While at the university, I got my first job as a choreographer for a dance team. It was there that I met Nicu Ceausescu, who worked in the same building. A lot has been said over the years about my "relationship" with Nicu, President Nicolae Ceausescu's son. Even you asked if I was his girlfriend toward the end of my gymnastics career and later, when I worked as a coach for the government. It is one of the tamer questions I've been asked about Nicu.

I can say that Nicu and I were acquaintances and that he seemed to be a nice guy. It has been written that he was a wild drinker and a womanizer. I don't know if any of that was true. What I heard is that he helped a lot of people. Many mysteries surround him, but it is not my place to judge. People gossip; they are interested only in the bad things, the mistakes others make. It is human nature to try to knock down anyone the public perceives as having climbed too high. Nicu was born to an elevated position. He was Nicolae's son, and for that, he paid a very high price, especially toward the end of his life.

I have never talked in detail about Nicu because there isn't much to say. I'm not interested in the speculations about our so-called relationship, and I hope that you will respect that. People speculated about us because we were seen at some of the same receptions and parties, but there were always ten or twenty other people there, too, and we were never alone. So, let me make this very clear—Nicu and I were never boyfriend and girlfriend.

During those early years in Bucharest, I didn't date anyone very seriously, though the media had me engaged to an assortment of men. I'd go out and have a good time, but when I realized a relationship wasn't going to go that far, I'd stop it right there. I could always tell when something wasn't going to work. Prospective boyfriends would ask what had happened, what they'd done wrong . . . and I couldn't tell them exactly. It was just a feeling that things weren't going to work and that we should move on. With my husband, Bart, things were different. People say that in your life, you have one big love. Bart Conner is mine. My destiny was to be with him, but it took defecting and a lot of hard knocks before we ever truly met.

But back to my first coaching job. I did choreography for a folk-dance troupe. After years of learning the intricate choreography and dance steps for my floor routines, I was well qualified for the job. I made a little bit of money, and for the first time in my life, I felt like an adult. Occasionally, I'd have neighbors over for some drinks. We Romanians like to party. We like life, and we live life. We never think ten days from a given moment because we know the world is so uncertain. In those days, if there was food on the table and something to drink, we were happy. In a Communist system, you never know what tomorrow will bring. Things can change overnight. You have to take your fun when you can.

In 1981, I received a telephone call from the Gymnastics Federation, telling me that a group of Romanian gymnasts was going to the United States to do an exhibition tour. The government wanted to raise $250,000 from the eleven-city show. They offered me $1,000 to join the group. For me, that was a lot of money (I made about $3 a day at my job), and I needed it, so I agreed to go. Since the government sponsored my job, there was no difficulty getting time off for the trip. And the government was going to make money on me, so the officials were naturally very supportive of my decision.

Bela and Marta, I was told, would be leading the tour. Whatever trouble Bela had been in after the 1980 Olympics, it seemed he was out of it by then. The director of the Gymnastics Federation would also be on the tour as head of the delegation, along with several undercover policemen (introduced to everyone as journalists), sent to make certain that nothing went wrong. The director was going to be in charge of our schedules, hotels, transportation, and even our passports. I would be allowed to govern my own time a bit . . . mostly because the tour was called "Nadia '81." Without me, it wouldn't have happened.

I remember the best part of the trip was that we got to ride a bus with a group of American gymnasts. None of the Romanians could speak English very well, but we had a great time with the cute, blond guys. We listened to their music and tried to communicate, even though we didn't speak the same language. I spoke a lot to Kurt Thomas but remember thinking that another gymnast, Bart Conner, was cute. He bounced around the bus talking to everyone—he was incredibly friendly and fun.

I was not that unhappy in Romania when I went on the tour—my hardships were no more or less than anyone else's in my country. It never crossed my mind that I would ever live anywhere else in the world. Defection was not in my thoughts. I finally had a job and the adult life I'd craved for so long. Yes, I was poor, but I was getting used to it by then. Everyone was poor; everyone struggled. And I loved my country. I still do. When I went on the exhibition tour, I didn't know how unhappy Bela and Marta were (their school in Deva had lost most of its government support). But I will get to that later. Suffice it to say that I probably had more fun on that tour than I had during any other . . . until the end.

Bela recalls that he was forced to accompany the team on its tour, despite the fact that he was no longer the national team coach. He did not want to go because he was disgusted with the government and its treatment of him after the Olympics, but the director gave him no choice. He was also forbidden to speak to any foreign media. After his comments to the ABC reporter, the government was not taking any chances with him. Bela felt like the entire tour was a humiliation.

Throughout the tour, I reported to the director when I wanted to do anything or go anywhere. He was fairly lenient with me, but I was always accompanied on my outings by one of our "journalists." Still, I was allowed out to discos with the guys, as long as I didn't do anything dangerous (the director believed someone might want to kidnap me). I was given a long leash. At the time, I didn't realize that a long leash was still a leash or that it might tighten until I felt strangled.

What happened next is a blur. I can only tell you what I myself know for certain, which is that there was a big fight between Bela and the director. The outcome was that Bela, Marta, and Geza Pozsar, our choreographer, believed they had no choice but to defect from Romania because they feared for their lives and their families' safety. In a single night, the course of their lives changed forever.

My friend, you asked me about courage and the Olympics, and I have told you about the Karolyis' decision because it puts your question into perspective. To decide the course of your life and that of your family in one night, with no assurance of success, is unfathomable. Nine years later, I would know more about true courage when I, too, decided to defect. But I sometimes wonder, to this day, if courage is just another word for desperation.

The Scream

A great floor exercise is composed of five ingredients. First, the gymnast must have secure landings on all of the tumbling skills. Second, she needs good height on her skills, both for high scores and for safety. Third, she has to have endurance because if she runs out of gas before her last tumbling run, she's in big trouble. Fourth, the gymnast must have great conditioning so that she can avoid injuries. And fifth, she must be able to sell her routine to the judges and audience by presenting her choreography well.

I was walking along the road with two friends.
The sun was setting.
I felt a breath of melancholy —
Suddenly the sky turned blood-red.
I stopped, and leaned against the railing, deathly
    tired —
Looking out across the flaming clouds that hung
    like blood and a sword
Over the blue-black fjord and town.

> *My friends walked on—I stood there, trembling*
> *   with fear.*
> *And I sensed a great, infinite scream pass through*
> *   nature.*

—Entry in Edvard Munch's diary, 1892

Friend, have you ever seen Edvard Munch's painting *The Scream*? A man stands on a road lined by a diagonal railing. His mouth is open, gaping; his hands are raised to his head; his eyes stretch wide and appear tormented and haunted. In the background are two men in top hats, and behind them is the landscape of Oslo—hills and valleys. I have read that in *The Scream*, Munch was trying to portray a state of mind. Can you imagine being caught in a person's scream? Can you comprehend a moment of such total horror, insanity, and dread? I can.

The first time I saw that painting, I knew it. Really knew it. The man is a prisoner, and he will never escape the cell Munch painted him in; he will never be free. I imagine that is how Bela, Marta, and Geza felt when they realized that they were trapped by a lie, when they accepted that they had no choice but to defect from their country. Perhaps they, too, screamed, but the sound came from deep inside their souls, and they couldn't let it out for fear that they would be caught and taken back to Romania in handcuffs.

From your last letter, I don't think you understand what it means to be without your country. You have written that you've traveled a bit in Europe, but English is a common language in most countries. The Romanian language is not. Plus, you have always had a return ticket to your home, have you not? You have left your city, family, neighbors, and way of life but known all the while that in two weeks time, you'd return, pick up your mail, go to the grocery store, and dine with friends. You have a U.S. passport and can travel anywhere in the world, regardless of your country's affiliations or status or whether your government approves. And you can always return.

When the Karolyis and Geza decided to defect, they knew that they could never go back to their homeland. They left behind their families and friends, their homes, and all of their belongings. They left with the tiny suitcases they'd brought on our exhibition tour and the clothes on their backs. No pictures; no mementos of Romania; no command of the English language; no dear friends in the United States; no certainty that they wouldn't be denied permission to stay and be sent back home to certain imprisonment for the crime of defection.

You've asked how I felt when I learned of Bela's defection plans. You are right to assume that he told me about them but incorrect in the assumption that I was desperate to join him. In 1981, I couldn't imagine facing the overwhelming challenges of defection. And I had no idea what was happening in the lives of my coaches and choreographer until the last night of the tour. But let me tell you how the situation played out.

Bela recalls saying good-bye to all of us during a morning meeting on our last day in Manhattan. The gymnasts were scheduled for several hours of shopping before returning to the hotel and taking a bus to the airport. He told the girls that they were great athletes and that they could maintain their careers by hard work and discipline, and he gave them all hugs. I don't recall that morning. All I remember is that the night before

Bela defected, I ran into him in the hallway of our hotel. It was late, and I was going to my room to pack. We were alone, and Bela said softly that he was thinking of not going back. I thought he was joking or that he might be checking to see if I was thinking of defection so that he could stop me. "Whatever," I said with a smile and went to my room. I had been trained for so many years not to react to anything that what Bela said didn't register as being even possibly for real.

The next morning was our last opportunity to shop in New York before returning home, and all of the gymnasts were excited. I ran into Bela before I set off, and he mentioned again that he was thinking of not going back. Once more, I ignored the idea and its implications. When I returned from the stores, I went to my room to finish packing. We had a team meeting at noon, and Bela, Marta, and Geza weren't there. I assumed they were still shopping. I went to my room, and the telephone rang. It was a woman who said, "Bela asked me to call and see if you want to stay in the United States or return to Romania." "I am going home," I replied and hung up the phone.

I don't think I really even considered the woman's question. I had grown up in a Communist country, and I knew nothing else. My family lived in Romania—how could I ever think of leaving them? Sure, life was tough, but wasn't it tough everywhere? Remember, I never saw enough of any of the places we traveled to to get the idea that "real" people didn't struggle like we did. It was not worth throwing away what I knew for the unknown.

In the minutes following that phone call, the reality sank in. I sat down on my hotel room bed and felt a wave of cold travel from my toes to my head. My God, is this actually happening? Could it really be true? I went down to the front desk to ask for Bela's room key. The clerk refused to give it to me, but I told him that I had left something in Bela's room and needed to pack it in my suitcase before we left. I stressed how important it was to get into the room, and he finally gave me the key. It felt sharp and dangerous in my hand.

The walk to Bela's room felt unbearably long. When I opened the door, the room was empty. The Karolyis were gone, and suddenly, I knew that it was completely true: They had defected. Friend, you think I was dense for not accepting Bela's initial words, but in Romania at that time, a person couldn't even trust her own shadow. I respected and loved Bela, but I lived according to the unspoken rule of my country: Trust no one completely. But Bela had trusted me. I was the only person he told about his decision to defect. If I had been older and wiser, I would have understood, and I would have trusted him, too.

By 3:00 P.M. when the gymnasts boarded the bus, it became clear to everyone that the Karolyis and Geza had disappeared. The director told us that their passports were missing; he was in charge of everyone's, so somehow Bela must have stolen them from his room. On the plane, he told me that the defection was not that important because "the Queen" was still with him and was going home. By "the queen," he meant me. The director said that if I hadn't returned with him, he would have been decapitated.

I cried a little on the plane ride, mostly because I wondered what would happen to all of the young gymnasts in Deva. I was grown up, but they were still little girls and depended on the Karolyis and Geza. I cried a

bit for myself, too. Bela and Marta had been parental fig-
ures in my life, and I would miss them. Still, I never
worried about them because it wasn't as if they'd been
kidnapped. They'd decided to defect, and as a result of
all of the disagreements Bela had had with the Gymnastics Federation and high-ranking government officials,
he was probably better off. His opportunities in Romania had faded, and he was losing ground. It was time for
a new life and a second chance.

It was a quiet journey home. You could almost hear
all of the officials thinking about what they were going
to tell their superiors concerning the defections. No
doubt, they would all be reprimanded and possibly de-
moted. Ceausescu would be furious because having well-
known people defect made Romania look bad. During
the long flight, most of the officials put pen to paper and
tried to figure out what they were going to report. I was
glad that I was not in their position.

My life drastically changed after the Karolyis defected. I was no longer allowed to travel outside Romania. I wasn't even allowed to go to Moscow. Whenever
the Gymnastics Federation put me on a list to travel for
some kind of exhibition tour, the list came back with my
name crossed out. Every single time, I was cut from the
list. Perhaps the government thought that because Bela
defected, I eventually would as well. But I'd had my
chance in New York, and I hadn't taken it. I wouldn't
leave my brother, who depended on me. I couldn't leave
my mother and father or my country.

Being treated like a traitor was extremely upsetting,
and I couldn't find any answers as to why I was in that
position. Nobody was willing to ask any high-ranking
officials why my wings had been clipped: If you asked

questions, you might get fired. I called the director and asked why someone in the government didn't want me to travel. But the director knew only that someone very high up had ordered that nobody should "bother" to put my name on any invitations because I was not allowed to travel anymore. Everyone was told that I was "busy, busy, busy." I wasn't.

Life, my friend, took on a new bleakness. I was cut off from making the small amount of extra money that had really made the difference in my family's life. It was also insulting that a normal person in Romania had the chance to travel whereas I could not. I kept wondering, why me? Some people were laughing in my face—"Look at you, the big deal Nadia Comaneci, and you can't even make a trip to London."

When my gymnastics career was over, there was no longer any need to keep me happy. I was to do as I was instructed, just as I'd done my entire life. I was expected to keep sacrificing. After everything that had gone before, it was humiliating. If Bela hadn't defected, I would still have been watched, but his defection brought a spotlight on my life, and it was blinding. I started to feel like a prisoner. In reality, I had always been one. If a country does not allow freedom, even if the chains are invisible, you are still a prisoner. Inside, I started to scream, but the sound was soft and I could still ignore it.

Several years passed, with each day, week, and month much like the last, and I graduated with my sports diploma and was given a new job within the Gymnastics Federation. It was my responsibility to go to different clubs in Bucharest, Deva, and other cities and to see what the gymnasts were doing. Then I'd bring back a report about the coaching and training facilities. I had a great relationship with everyone and enjoyed the job, but it was nothing special. I was like any other person who gets a salary. The government still took a percentage out of my paycheck each month for my mortgage. I never thought about asking for a raise because the officials would have thought I'd lost my mind.

In 1984, I was still making about the same amount I'd made while I was at the university. The government was not obligated to pay me more than I'd made in my previous job. The only way I was going to increase my salary was to be named to a very high position, maybe as president of the Gymnastics Federation. But that wasn't going to happen because someone directly under Ceausescu would have to appoint me to the position, and that person was probably the very person who had dictated that I could no longer travel.

To add insult to injury, when I reached my twenty-fifth birthday, the government started taking a large portion of money out of my salary each month because I didn't have any children—something they did to all women that age without offspring. Sounds strange, doesn't it? But it is true. You have asked to know more about Ceausescu and his arbitrary laws, and I am pleased that you inquired. To understand our former president is to comprehend why Romania became a ravaged country.

Before I tell you about our deposed leader, let me reiterate that I never personally knew Ceausescu or his wife. I met them one time when I was a child, and we spoke only a few words at an official ceremony. It makes me uncomfortable to judge them in any way because who am I to know? So I must look to the history books and well-known journalists for answers, not rumors, so that I can do justice to your questions and be fair to Ceausescu and his descendants.

According to the history books, Ceausescu and his wife, Elena Petrescu, came from a background in the Communist Party. Ceausescu ran Romania's Ministry of Agriculture and was deputy minister of the armed forces when the Communists took power in our country. He worked his way through the ranks and became the president of Romania in 1974. From the start, he ran the country with an iron fist, controlling the media by using the Securitate, his secret police.

Political insiders have reported that Ceausescu and his wife ran the country together. It is written that Elena collected titles (all bestowed by her husband, not earned) like diamonds and loved to wear both. She received a Ph.D. in industrial chemistry and was appointed to the National Council of Scientific Research despite knowing nothing about the field. She was a member of the Permanent Bureau of the Political Executive Committee; as first deputy premier, she supervised the secret police and launched programs such as the antireligion and antiabortion campaigns. Elena also helped decide who would be promoted within the government. Some say she was more powerful than the president and far crueler. In any case, the Ceausescus' rule in its entirety was bizarre and brutal.

During the mid-1970s, Ceausescu decided that Romania's population should increase from 23 million to 30 million by the year 2000. He wanted more followers, more tax dollars, a more powerful country. To this end, he created a policy that said, "The fetus is the property of the entire society. Anyone who avoids having children is a deserter who abandons the laws of national continuity."

Abortion was forbidden, and people like me who didn't have children by the age of twenty-five were monetarily penalized for not doing our patriotic duty.

It's been documented that under Ceausescu's so-called fetus policy, Romania's birthrate doubled, but we didn't have the food or nutrients necessary to either feed the new children or maintain the health of pregnant women. Ceausescu forbade sex education and any books on reproduction and had them classified as "state se-crets." Women under forty-five were forced to go to clinics every three months to see if they were pregnant. The government officials who took them to these ap-pointments were called the "menstrual police." I never had to go. Perhaps my status was good for something after all.

Friend, I've tried to explain to you that there simply wasn't enough food in Romania for its inhabitants. By 1981, things went from bad to horrific. Our country could have survived on our farmlands and livestock, but Ceausescu exported most of our food. He had incurred $10 billion in loans from the West and decided in 1981 that he was going to pay the debt in full by exporting everything that could be sold abroad. As a result, the people were given food rations of 1 to 2 pounds of meat a month. That's not enough for an individual for a week, let alone a family of five. People could have stopped hav-ing children . . . but they couldn't afford to. Plus, failing to reproduce was a crime.

Ceausescu kept spending—building shipping canals that were never used; buying lavish homes (he owned forty); and allowing his wife to spend millions on jew-elry, yachts, and travel. Meanwhile, in many cities there wasn't enough electricity to boil hot water more than once a day. Articles state that Ceausescu forced people in factories to work seven-day weeks and cut their pay at the same time. He decided to "redevelop" land and displaced thousands from their homes. He didn't care about preserving the culture, and he forbade religion, which was all most people had for comfort.

I didn't know any of these details while I was living in Romania because our media were subject to Ceausescu's whims and desires. To this day, I can't say for certain exactly what is true, so I must depend upon the same books and articles that you do. I didn't grow up hating Ceausescu, but I knew the hardships of living in Romania and admit that I was not surprised to learn of the cruelties he and his wife perpetrated or the thousands they crippled through overwork, starvation, and countless inhuman acts. I witnessed the results of the president and first lady's laws. Beggars panhandled on the streets of every city, people starved while our eggs and beef were exported, beautiful churches were demolished, and children died. Still, I did not think of defecting.

In 1984, I heard rumors that there was going to be a boycott of the summer Olympics to be held in Los Angeles, California. Many Communist nations, including the Soviet Union, Cuba, and East Germany, decided to retaliate for the U.S.-led boycott of the 1980 Games by refusing to compete in the 1984 Los Angeles Olympics. I don't know why Ceausescu didn't join them in this boycott, but probably one of the best decisions he made in his life was to let the athletes who had trained so hard compete.

In our country, we were told that as a reward for Ceausescu permitting Romanians to compete, some kind of agreement had been struck between the United

States and our government so that if any Romanians tried to defect during the Games, they would be sent home. I don't know if that is true, but not one individual defected during those Olympics. Most of the time, *somebody* out of a huge delegation failed to return home. The rumor could have been propaganda put out by our government. Either way, it worked, as no one wanted to end up facing the Securitate. Everyone was too afraid.

I did not think that the 1984 Olympics would involve me. There was no way I would be allowed to travel to the United States when I wasn't even allowed to go to Europe. But I received a phone call from a government official saying that I would be part of the Romanian delegation. I remember staring at the phone I held in shock because I couldn't believe the government was actually going to let me get on a plane! I was assigned a "chaperone" for the trip, but I really didn't care that I was going to be watched. I was traveling to America, and I planned to eat, shop, and meet as many fun people as possible. For a brief moment, I felt almost free.

Officially, I went with the Romanian delegation to the Olympics as a spectator. I watched Bela's newest creation, Mary Lou Retton, and she was great. From a distance, I saw Bela, and I was later permitted to say hello but not to talk to him. Even if I'd found myself alone with Bela for a few minutes, I would have been too afraid to speak anyway. Do you know what that kind of crippling fear is like? If my mother had been in that arena and I'd been dying to talk to her, I still wouldn't have tried because someone would have taken off my head if they found out I'd had a forbidden conversation. I had no control over what the Romanian delegation officials might write about me. I felt that I needed to keep everyone pleased and happy; I couldn't rock the boat.

Can you understand that this kind of behavior—always watching what I said and did—had become automatic for me? If I didn't open my mouth, people couldn't make up anything about me. So, I didn't say a word. I became disinterested in even speaking, let alone speaking my mind or having an unscripted, authentic moment. I knew my phone and the rental car and my hotel room were all bugged. My chaperone, a middle-aged woman who'd had a government job all her life and never thought outside the box, and the delegation officials took notes on every move I made. It was an unnerving, pressure-filled situation.

I was pleased, though, to see that Bela and Marta had landed on their feet in the United States. The idea that they'd applied what they'd learned and taught in Romania to gymnasts in America made me proud. In a way, I was a small piece of that success. After a few weeks, I returned to Romania a little happier for the break I'd had and went back to the same job. Once more, life was about surviving, taking care of my brother, and keeping my home at least partially heated for the winter. I got back into the swing of not really going anywhere and being just another worker bee. Sometimes I still wanted to scream, but other times I just moved through life in a self-protective haze.

My friend, there are moments in life when you lose your edge, so to speak. Even though there's a small voice inside you that is desperately trying to shake you out of the haze, it's hard to hear it. Try to always listen to that voice because it speaks the truth, even when you don't want to hear what it's saying. Sometimes it's easier to go through the motions of life than to actually live it. I always remind myself that a life worth living is one full of awareness, actions, and choices.

Even in the bleakest of my days, stories reached my ears. I heard about a man who'd traveled to America through France, Spain, and Cádiz in a freight container, only to be deported back to Romania on the same ship on which he'd hidden. Ten days later, he tried again, over the same route, winding up in the Canary Islands. In the end, it took him a year and four months to go back to Italy and then to France before he finally arrived in the United States.

For every person who made it, I heard about countless others who did not—who were deported, jailed indefinitely, or shot in the back while running across the border. I heard about a group of people who lived in a freight container in the bottom of a ship in an attempt to defect. These were desperate people willing to die in an attempt to find a better life. Life as you know it has to be pretty bad in order for you to nail yourself into a freight container and suffer through an ocean crossing without knowing if you'll be successful.

You have asked what the exact moment was when I finally decided to defect. I cannot tell you. There were so many factors, based on so many years of struggle, humiliation, and hardship. Would I have even considered it if I'd been allowed to travel freely or if I'd been given a job with decent pay? Probably not. But one day, I realized that where I was in life was where I was going to die. There were no opportunities in my country for advancement unless I wanted to be a savvy political player, and that was not in my nature. I could not hope for a better job or more money or the opportunity to see the world as a gymnastics delegation member. I couldn't even decide what to cook for dinner because there were no groceries to buy. One day, I just realized that I'd reached a dead end. I realized that I could either be like all of those people silently screaming around me or give myself permission to have a voice, to decide how my life should go.

I understand that to Americans, the idea that there is no choice is hard to believe. Have you ever had a disturbing dream from which you could not wake yourself? Or been caught in a strong current and watched the land pass by without being able to get to the shore? That is what living in Romania as an adult under Ceausescu was like for me. One day, I realized that I wanted my own dreams, that I desperately wanted to swim for the distant shore and sink my feet into its sand. I finally heard myself scream, and I listened.

The process of defection began when I attended a birthday party at a friend's home. At the party were several Romanians who had defected and were now U.S. citizens. One of them said he lived in Florida, where the sun never stopped shining, there were palm trees everywhere, and the ocean water was crystal clear and warm year-round. He also said he'd helped his cousin get out of Romania by swimming across the Danube and insinuated that he'd assisted others and would continue to do so. The man was of medium height and had brown hair and a mustache. He seemed nice, and he was believable because he was now an American. His name was Constantin.

My conversation with Constantin was casual, but I remember telling my brother about it later. I pulled him into a room and played some loud music so that I could be sure we wouldn't be overheard. I was convinced that my house was bugged. "I think this is going to have to stop," I told Adrian. "My life is bad." Adrian just listened. "I heard a man talking," I explained. "He said he could help people defect . . . he didn't ask if I wanted to leave Romania, but I think I do." My brother was quiet for a long time, and then he looked me in the eyes and agreed that it was time for a change. He understood that I needed to leave Romania to find a better life.

Fairy Tales

My typical floor tumbling runs included a round-off back handspring, and a double back somersault in tucked position. A round-off to a one-half turn to a piked front somersault (called a "piked Arabian"), a step-out to a round-off back handspring lay-out back somersault, landing with legs straddled. And a round-off back handspring and back flip with a double twist. The most difficult skill was the double back somersault. Only a handful of gymnasts in the world did the double back consistently.

My friend, when you were a young child, did you ever read Walt Disney's *Sleeping Beauty*? It's about a princess, Aurora, who is cursed by an evil fairy named Maleficent. According to the curse, Aurora would prick her finger on a spindle on her sixteenth birthday and die. But good fairies, determined to save her, changed the curse so that when the princess pricked her finger, she would fall into a deep sleep, only to awaken after the first kiss of her true love.

We had a folktale in Romania that was very similar. I used to imagine I was Sleeping Beauty, just waiting to meet my prince, have him kiss me, and then wake to find myself in a castle. The only thing was, there were no princes in Romania. And even if they'd existed, they wouldn't have looked for me in a house with little heat or at a job in a dusty old government building. I was warehoused and invisible, and life appeared utterly hopeless. Meeting Constantin made me feel as if a window had been cracked open, and suddenly, a fresh breeze carried the promise of a different future than the one to which I'd resigned myself.

When I began to fantasize about defection, my mind came alive, and it seemed that almost anything was possible. I was like a thirsty person in the desert—all of a sudden, I realized that, somewhere, there was a glass of water. I had to survive traveling through the desert to hold it in my hand . . . but it was there. And freedom was there, too, if I was willing to risk everything to attain it. But was I?

My brother asked if he could meet Constantin. We went together at the next opportunity for a "friendly" gathering that wouldn't make anyone in the Securitate suspicious. Constantin told Adrian that he knew of a way for me to get out of Romania. He had a friend with some family close to the border with Hungary. He suggested we visit that family for a party and get the government used to my socializing with people who lived by the border. If I just went one time, it would cause suspicion. But if I went and returned several times, it might result in a more lax attitude on the part of the police and give both me and the handful of other Romanians who planned to defect with Constantin enough time to cross the border before an alarm was sounded.

When my brother finished the conversation, he told me that Constantin was the real deal. He wasn't bluffing. There were six other Romanians who planned to trust him with their lives. "There is nothing left for you in this country," Adrian said. "The way you are treated by the government is humiliating. If you want to defect, you should try." That meant so much, knowing that he wanted me to be happy despite how much he'd miss me.

I agreed to go visit Constantin's friends near the border. That's when I met the other six people who wanted to defect—two women and four men, one of whom had tried to defect three times and failed. The man who had repeatedly failed had made it to Hungary, but authorities there had sent him back. There was no guarantee just because you'd crossed into Hungary that you'd be allowed to stay there. At the time, the Hungarian officials would look at your intellect, your skills, and your ability to contribute to their society, and if you were considered valuable and productive, you could stay. If not, back to Romania with you. The man I met had been jailed when he'd been returned. Yet still he wanted to attempt defection for a fourth time.

The idea of freedom solidified into something real and terrifying and thrilling. Meanwhile, I couldn't tell my mother and father anything about my plans. If I had told them, it would have put them in danger, and I was not willing to take that risk in exchange for some comforting words. Secretly, I began to put my papers in order. I placed my home in my brother's name so that he and his wife wouldn't lose it if I successfully defected. The government would have turned them out on the street had I left the house in my name. We just crossed our fingers that the paperwork we did would protect Adrian.

I still wasn't certain I could actually do it. I continued to go to "parties" at the home of Constantin's friends. Since the house was so close to a border, police monitored the neighborhood. In order to enter, we had to sign in at a security gate and then sign out when we left. While there, we played music, chatted about nothing in particular, and tried to figure out if we trusted everyone in the group. The Securitate could have put one of their own into the mix and told him or her to pretend to defect so that they could catch us "criminals."

My brother and sister-in-law accompanied me every time I went to the house. Eventually, they started to wonder whether they, too, should defect. I told them to think hard because if we were caught, we'd all be on the streets. At least they had each other and a home. In the end, they decided that it was too much of a risk and that they weren't quite unhappy enough to take it. Do you understand, dear friend, how desperate a person must be to attempt defection? I had to weigh the value of seeking a better life against the probability of my imprisonment or death if I failed in the effort.

Each time I went to a "party," I made certain to let the secret police know my exact plans by talking about them in public. That way, they believed they were still in complete control of my comings and goings. The others did the same. None of us wanted to attract attention, but it was necessary to defect close to the border if we had any hope of getting across it, and that house was at the beginning of our journey. Maybe we would get a bullet in the back before we'd gone 100 yards; maybe death would come only seconds before crossing the border. But like those that had tried before us, we were all desperate enough to risk dying. In the end, it didn't come down to trusting the other would-be defectors or Constantin. I understood fairy tales were just children's stories. I simply wanted more out of my life.

On my last visit to the house by the border, I failed to go back through the police gate. Instead, I ran forward into darkness.

Defection

My beam routine at the 1976 Olympics: I started by facing the side of the beam, then jumped to a straddle L position and pressed to a handstand and a one-quarter pirouette step down to stand on the beam. Next, an artistic step-step to gainer back handspring to three-quarter turn. Two steps to the end of the beam to an aerial front walkover, side-kick, and turn. Side aerial cartwheel to immediate back handspring, then choreography. From a seated position, back walkover through handstand to standing position (called a "Valdez"). Split leap from end of beam, back walkover to two back handsprings. Choreography and poses to two steps into a cartwheel to immediate back flip with a double twist dismount.

In your last letter, young friend, you treated my decision to defect with respect. Yet I am troubled by the feeling that you lack a full understanding of what exactly it meant. Have you truly grasped how dangerous it was to think outside of the government's rules and laws? How insane it was to even try to defect? How far Ceausescu could reach?

All of the what-ifs barreled through my head like a train. What if my parents were hurt because of my decision to defect? What if my brother, despite our best efforts, still lost my house and had to live on the street? What if my family members were imprisoned by the secret police, interrogated, tortured? It's the what-ifs that wear you down and make you afraid to move. Romania's government officials counted on that. Their ability to spread fear and paralyze the people of our country is now well documented.

So, what gave me the courage to slip out of that house on the border and into the night? Everything I'd done, heard, spoken, experienced, yearned for, suffered through, desired, required, hoped, and dreamed. Everything blotted out the nothingness of my existence. I prayed my parents would be well, for I'd left them out of my scheme, and that my brother would remain untouched. I prayed that I would be able to move one foot in front of the other when I watched my six companions become shadows with pale, anxious faces and labored breath.

There was no way, of course, that my disappearance would go unnoticed. I had a government job and was expected to be at work every day. I'd been at work every day for eight years. If I didn't show up or call in sick, the alarm would sound because countless people would notice my absence. Time would be of the essence, and so, before my final visit to the house near the border, I had a farewell dinner at a restaurant in a nearby village with my brother and sister-in-law. We knew that the meal needed to be a public one and appear like any other so that no one watching us would be suspicious.

It was unbearably sad and difficult to pretend to enjoy a meal with my loved ones when I knew that, a few hours later, I might die. There was such concern and worry in Adrian's eyes that night. He knew only that our group was going to try to cross the border into Hungary but not exactly when or how or what would happen to his big sister if I was blessed enough to be successful. When dinner was finished, I stood up and walked away from my brother and his wife without looking back. I sincerely believed it was the last time I would ever see them in my life. But if I had looked back, I don't think I would have had the courage to go ahead with my plans. Regardless, I actually felt a piece of my heart breaking.

There was no plan. Constantin told our group that night that we were to follow the man who'd previously defected three times, through six hours of icy terrain, half-frozen lakes, and dense woods and across the Hungarian border. It was November, and the temperature was below zero, so we would have to move quickly to keep from getting hypothermia. Constantin would wait for us across the border in a car. We would try to sleep through the night somewhere and then decide individually if we wanted to present ourselves at the Hungarian embassy and ask for asylum.

The man who had attempted defection gave our group some last-minute advice before we stepped out of the house into the night and began our run for the border. "No flashlights," he instructed, "there are guards everywhere, and the light will give us away. If you hear a noise behind you, don't run. If it's a guard, he'll shoot you for running. If we get caught, don't run. Guards will also shoot you if you try to get away. Try to move silently, and don't talk."

When we stepped out into the night, we each put our hands on the shoulders of the person in front of us because once we moved away from the house, it was impossible to see. If I hadn't been touching the person in front of me, I would have gotten separated from the group and been lost. I remember that the ground beneath my feet was icy and that I slipped again and again. Time moved so slowly that it seemed to stop. There was only the cold, the trudging and running when possible, and always the straining of my ears to hear a guard's call, the crunch of his boots, the click of his gun being readied.

I tried to think about anything but a bullet in my back. We reached a frozen lake that didn't appear too solid. It wasn't, but the water seemed shallow, and there was nowhere else to cross. As soon as we all put our weight on the ice, it cracked and we fell into knee-deep water. It was cold as hell. Please, God, I thought, just let me make it to the other side without the bottom of the lake getting deeper and the water going over my head. I wouldn't have lasted two minutes submerged in that freezing lake. It took a long time to get across the water, but the pain of cold blocked out everything else. We were numb.

Many times during the next six hours, I was overwhelmed by the gravity of what I was doing. I couldn't believe I'd actually made the decision to defect, that I was risking my life, that I'd never see my parents or brother again. But I never thought of turning back. Where was I going to go? Back to my house, where I could barely afford the heat? Back to a dead-end job and being treated as if I had never done anything to bring my country glory? Back to no future? Wasn't that the same as being dead?

There were many times when I didn't trust the man leading us. He said if we didn't "keep to the left," we'd end up back in Romania. Keep to the left . . . what kind of direction was that? I wanted to see a compass or a map or something. But there was nothing to do in the dark except follow the guy and hope he knew where he was going. He told us that when we crossed 5 meters of very dark dirt, we were at the border. But we crossed a lot of dirt, and still there was no border. This is so stupid, I actually remember thinking. I'm going to get killed and all because I'm following a man with no sense of direction. I didn't say anything, though, because no one could break the silence and speak. I just concentrated on keeping my teeth from chattering.

There are many places along borders that are not lined with barbed-wire fences and have no guards. A country simply cannot control every square inch of its borders. We were supposed to cross into Hungary at one of those spots. Then our leader would guide us to a street where Constantin would be waiting in his car. But we never found the exact place where we were supposed to cross the border. We didn't find the street, let alone Constantin. We didn't even know we'd crossed into Hungary until we saw a small plaque that bore a long name with a lot of z's and s's. Clearly, not a Romanian name.

Our bedraggled group walked and walked and walked . . . right into two guards. Constantin had told us that, once in Hungary, if we encountered the police we were to say a single word that he'd taught us—*hello*, in Hungarian. The thing is, the guards went beyond hello and started asking questions, and we all looked at them like idiots. Plus, it was pretty suspicious to see a group of seven people walking down a deserted road at 2:00 A.M. Where the hell were we supposed to be going? The guards told us to go with them. They put us in a car and took us to the Hungarian police department. The car ride was silent. Not because we weren't allowed to talk but because every one of us was absolutely terrified.

Each of the potential defectors was interviewed separately. When the police saw my identification papers, they immediately offered to let me stay in Hungary. I was a famous gymnast and thus a hot catch in their minds. I think back on it now and wonder why I was so valuable to them. My career was over, and though I am considered a very good coach, what else could I really bring to Hungary? Two others in our group were also offered asylum. The rest were told that they'd be returned to Romania the following day. They began to cry.

"Look," I told the police, "I will only stay if the whole group is allowed to remain in your country." The words were out of my mouth before I even considered what might happen. Gymnastics had taught me to be a team player, and in this case, my team was made up of my fellow defectors. I just thought that the situation wasn't fair. We'd all taken the same risks and crossed the border, and we should all have been allowed to stay. "We came together, we'll stay together," I declared. To my complete surprise, the police agreed. Not only that, they offered us hotel accommodations for a week, until we got on our feet, and vouchers for food and help in finding jobs. I knew that we were not going to stay in Hungary, but we accepted the government's kindness because we were cold and hungry and desperately needed to sleep.

Meanwhile, Constantin, having realized that his plan had gone awry, found us just before we left the police station and told the police he'd take our group to the hotel. Instead, however, he chose a different one. He knew that the media and the police would soon find us, and he wanted to give us a little extra time to think before we made our next move. You see, my friend, Hungary was not our final destination. It was too close to Romania. We all planned to attempt to cross the Austrian border and seek asylum there.

We spent a sleepless night crammed together in one room. The next morning, I saw my picture on the front of a newspaper but couldn't read what the article said about me. I didn't need to read it, though. It was enough to know that I was already "missing" in Romania. Keep moving, I told myself, if you don't want the politics of defection to catch up and possibly result in the Hungarians handing you back to Romania. Later that morning, the group divided into two cars. Constantin drove one car, and his friend drove the other. We were going to try and cross the border into Austria.

It was a six-hour drive to the Austrian border. No one was following us or watching either car. We were one step ahead of the Hungarians and Romanians. At the border, the Austrians stopped cars randomly to check for identification papers. Constantin decided to leave us at a café while he drove through to see whether he would be stopped. When he returned, he told us that he had, in fact, been stopped and that it was too dangerous to try to drive across the border with us. We would have to cross at another spot . . . at night.

What can I say of that moment? You just go on. The idea of another night crossing wasn't high on my list, but what else could I do? Constantin once again said he'd be waiting just on the other side of the border. I had to trust that he would be there because there were no alternatives. In gymnastics, I could kind of control my destiny—if I did well, I'd be rewarded with the esteem of my country.

But life is another story, and the process of dehumanization in Romania and the perils and uncertainties of defection showed me just how little control I had over the circumstances of my life.

Constantin told us where to cross the border. We waited for darkness to settle and then began to walk. I was more frightened than the first time, probably because I was closer to my goals and because to have them snatched away at this point would have been more devastating than getting caught in Romania. Stay in control, I told myself. Focus on your breathing and being silent and not getting lost. Focus on staying alive. There were seven barbed-wire fences to climb, and though I don't remember feeling their bite, my body was covered by cuts from the sharp metal. I'm incredibly coordinated, but there's no way to avoid getting cut by barbed wire. Most of the group was covered with blood. It took about two hours to get over all of those fences. I was exhausted when we saw the road where Constantin was supposed to pick us up. He'd instructed us to stay hidden on the side of the asphalt because there might be police cars passing by. Constantin said that he planned to break one of the headlights on each car so we'd know when to come out of hiding.

We lay on our bellies, hidden by weeds, and watched each car pass by, straining to see one with a broken headlight. When we saw two in a row with only one headlight each, we leaped to our feet and piled into the cars. That night, all of us slept on the floor of a single hotel room. The atmosphere couldn't have been more different from that in the hotel in Hungary. We were celebrating. There was an air of relief and sheer joy in that room.

Once in Austria, everyone except for me was on his or her own. Most of the group went to a homeless shelter for refugees. They were given a place to live and sleep until someone came and offered them jobs. Once they were given work and had sponsors, they could apply to the government for citizenship. I was thankful that I wasn't on my own in a foreign country where I couldn't speak the language. Constantin stayed with me and took me to the American embassy. He knew that I wanted to go to the United States, and he seemed very willing to help me get there.

It bothered me in your last letter that you just wanted me to tell you "the dirt" on Constantin. You've heard all the rumors, and maybe you believe that he controlled me, kept me a prisoner when I came to America, tried to make money off my defection. I will get to all of that and to what truth there is to the rumors. Remember that no one is purely good or evil; we all have a little bit of the angel and the devil in us. For now, let me tell you how things unfolded.

Constantin took me to the American embassy in Austria because I wanted to ask for political asylum. I remember walking through the doors and telling the first person I met that I was Nadia Comaneci and I wanted asylum. It created quite a spectacle and a flurry of activity. I felt like every paper had been dropped at the mention of my name. People in the embassy stared at me as if I were a ghost. An official told me that the people in the embassy had heard I'd defected but that no one knew where to find me. If I'd had the ability to communicate better, I would have told him that over the last few days, I didn't even know where I was myself.

"What do you want to do?" the official asked me.

"I want to go to America," I replied.

"When?"

"As soon as possible."

"There's a Pan Am flight leaving in two hours, you're on it," he said with a smile. I was considered a "person of special ability," which is a category for scientists, artists, and others who can contribute to American society; such people are fast-tracked through the system. Strange how hard defection had been until that moment, and then suddenly, the pieces slid into place. I thought I'd died and gone to heaven. Everything was going to be easy now, a veritable piece of cake. I'd fly to the United States and get a great job and make tons of money. The public would admire me for my past accomplishments, and I'd be rewarded in terms of my shining future goals. But if you believe that is how it happened, I have a bridge in Romania to sell you.

The embassy completed the necessary paperwork and then put me in a police car with an escort. The Pan Am personnel were extremely generous and seated me in first class on their flight. First class! I wouldn't have cared if they'd put me in the cargo hold. I was finally free, and I was on a flight to the United States of America. The fact that I was fed a lovely meal and given wine and champagne was just icing on a cake that was already iced.

I thought a lot about my brother during that flight. I wished that I could call him and tell him that I was safe. The Romanian government was probably saying that I was dead, with a bullet in my head. There was no way for me to contact him and tell him the truth. I also wondered, with the same lingering anxiety, what was going to happen when we landed in the United States.

Constantin told me that I was going to live with his wife and children for a bit. I never questioned him.

Please don't be like everyone else was, my friend: Don't tell me what I should have said to Constantin on the plane or what I should have done when I arrived in America. I'd spent my entire life being an object. When I was young, my coaches instructed me about how to train and live. The Gymnastics Federation decided if I was to compete or withdraw from competitions and exhibitions. The government moved me from place to place. I do not remember one moment when I lived as an entirely free person, when what I thought actually mattered, when I was given a voice. As an elite gymnast, every word I said to the Western media was scripted. Big brother watched and followed and listened. I had learned to live with secrets and mistrust and to keep my mouth shut.

I once read about a psychology experiment in which a dog is put in a cage with a bottom that can be triggered to electrically shock him. If the shock consistently comes from the left side, the dog learns to live on the right side. The reverse is true if the shock comes from the right side. But if the shock is inconsistent, coming from left or right randomly, the dog will eventually go crazy. I left Romania because I was going crazy. To learn that not everyone is as inconsistent as my government or the world of gymnastics or Ceausescu did not come easily to me when I arrived in America. I needed time to adjust.

Is it so unlikely that I would have done just as Constantin instructed on the plane, which was to trust him and follow his advice? Back then, I believed that if I listened to the instructions of the man in charge, I would have a better chance of survival. I also sincerely believed that the Romanian government would send someone to try to kill me. The officials would not let "their Nadia" defect because it would be an embarrassment to the country and a personal insult to Ceausescu. If I got hit by a car or fell off a tall building once I was in America, no one would question my death. I was sure that was how the secret police would do it.

When my plane landed in New York, people waiting for my arrival had packed a conference room at John F. Kennedy Airport. Following a ten-hour flight, I was rushed through customs and straight into a news conference. With Constantin at my side, I told reporters in my best English (which wasn't very good) that I knew life would be different in the United States but that "I was nine times in the States, I know the life here." Looking back, that statement wasn't just grammatically incorrect, it was horribly green. When asked how the Romanian government might feel about my defection, I said, "It's not my business."

Those statements were the beginning of my downfall in the eyes of many Americans. They thought I appeared cold and wooden. But consider that I'd just defected from my home and left behind everyone I loved. I'd trudged through freezing water and across icy fields and climbed over barbed-wire fences, all the while expecting to be shot. I'd prayed for asylum in Hungary and again in Austria, then I'd sat on a flight for ten hours next to a man I barely knew, contemplating a life that once again was out of my control. After all of that, I stepped into a room packed with journalists shouting questions and flashing cameras. Suffice it to say that I was shell-shocked.

You've asked if I knew that Constantin had a wife and four children at the time of that first news conference. I knew he was married, but the details didn't concern me, and that's what I told the media when they asked. My exact words were, "So what?" Constantin had offered to help me defect, and I'd accepted. I assumed that his wife knew that he was going help a handful of Romanians get out of the country and that I was one of them. But what people took from my two-word answer was that I was a home-wrecker. Nothing could have been further from the truth. In hindsight, I understand that I'd made a very poor choice of words.

Constantin had plans to become my personal manager upon our arrival in the United States. I didn't know that, but he'd promised to help me get settled, and I guess I just accepted his involvement in my future career as fair payment for the risks he'd taken. People died every day trying to defect. They drowned attempting to swim the Danube, got bullets in their backs for trying to cross the border, or risked suffocation in containers buried in the holds of ships bound for America. Some people believe Constantin kept me in a virtual prison, but I look at the situation a different way because he helped me come to the United States.

Friend, I will not apologize for my actions when I arrived in America. There are all sorts of excuses. I was in my late twenties, and I should have known better than to trust someone I didn't know. I wish I could take back the way I spoke, acted, and dressed. Of course, you remember all of the bad things—the harsh, overdone makeup; the fishnet stockings; and the short, tight skirts. I thought that was how I was supposed to look. The funny thing is, I thought I looked good. Don't you ever look back on pictures of yourself and wince?

Old friends in the United States—Bela Karolyi and Bart Conner—strained to learn news of my plans. They tried to contact me by telephone, but Constantin did not relay their messages. One day, Bart read in a newspaper article that I was scheduled to be on Pat Sajak's show. He recalls wondering both why I was going to do a mediocre talk show and why it was still impossible for any friends to contact me. Bart had worked as an announcer for NBC at the last Olympics, and he had a friend, Michael Weisman, who had been the executive producer of NBC Sports. Michael had moved on to be the head of late-night programming for CBS, which is the network that ran the Sajak show. Bart called Michael and asked about my scheduled appearance. I was set to appear that very night. They chatted about my defection and the fact that none of my old friends had been able to contact or see me.

"It would be great to have you on the show, too. Can you be in LA by 5:00 P.M.?" Michael asked. "We'll put you on the air."

"I don't know," Bart replied. "I'm in Oklahoma, but I'll check the flights and call you back."

Bart found a flight, grabbed a bag of clothes, and raced to the airport. He went for two reasons. First, he wanted to see if I needed any help. The press had been harsh about Constantin and me, and many old acquaintances thought something fishy was going on. Second, Bart knew that I might need work, and he had an established business in Oklahoma that could possibly support me. There was nothing romantic about his motivation. It was based on his desire to help a young woman he'd met once who was an icon in our shared sport.

Doing Time

The most difficult skills to learn on the beam are aerials. They are front and back flips without hands, and they're the toughest because a gymnast loses sight of the beam when flipping, so essentially she's working blind. But gymnasts develop an "air sense" on all of the apparatus pieces, especially the beam. Aerials become automatic because they're practiced thousands of times. An imaginary beam is created in a gymnast's mind, so even when she can't see it, she knows it's there. I always knew when I was crooked going into an aerial on the beam. Just like all elite gymnasts, I'd make tiny corrections while in the air. Those split-second judgments made the difference between falling off the beam and hurting myself or completing a successful skill that allowed me to win competitions.

When I found myself in Los Angeles on Pat Sajak's show, it was at one of my lowest moments. Today, I refuse to watch reruns of that interview because I hate the way I looked. People in Europe at the time dressed in short skirts and tiny tops, so that's what I was wearing. I wish I'd had somebody to teach me how to dress when I got to America. Constantin took me shopping because all I owned were a pair of jeans and the shirt on my back, but I only bought what I was used to wearing, which was a mistake. For that show, I wore a short, tight skirt and a big jacket. My makeup was way too thick, with too much blue eye shadow. Later, I learned that once you prove yourself and people like you, then you can essentially wear whatever you like in America. Until then, there are rules, and you must first gain credibility and respect before you break them.

I remember that I felt very trapped during that show. My English wasn't great, and I was afraid people wouldn't be able to understand me. Some say I came across as edgy and confrontational . . . I was really just scared. No one knew how it felt to be in my skin, and I was unable to communicate my unhappiness. I had no friends, and I felt lonely and terribly empty. Time, I reminded myself, will take care of everything, though I was finding that increasingly difficult to believe.

A few minutes before Bart Conner landed at the Los Angeles airport to surprise me on the Sajak show, he changed into nice clothes in the airplane bathroom, something you have to be a gymnast to be able to do. He was whisked by a CBS escort into a helicopter and flown to the studio, where the show was already in progress. The helicopter landed at CBS Television City. Bart ran through the back door, then someone slapped some powder on his face and handed him two dozen roses. "Welcome Nadia to America," he was told as they pushed him onto the stage where I sat talking to Pat Sajak.

"Nadia, you have an old friend here that wants to welcome you to the United States," Sajak said as Bart walked onto the set and handed me roses. I was speech-less. "Nadia, you guys have been friends a long time, right? When was the first time you met?" I told him it was in 1981 at the same time that Bart said it was in 1976. "Which is it?" Pat asked, laughing. "This is live TV, how close can you two be if you don't even known when you met? You're off by five years!"

Friend, I honestly remembered meeting Bart on the exhibition tour we did in 1981, but on live television, he reminded me about the American Cup in 1976 at Madi-son Square Garden. Bart had turned eighteen on the day of the competition, and the crowd sang "Happy Birth-day" to him. Both Bart and I won the competition and received silver cups that we were asked to pose with for the obligatory photo opportunity. A photographer then said, "Nadia's so cute, why don't you give her a kiss, Bart?" So Bart leaned over and gave me a little kiss on the cheek. It wasn't a romantic moment; he was eighteen and I was fourteen years old. But when Bart reminded me of that moment, I suddenly recalled it. "Oh, I do re-member a little blond guy," I said. Grinning, Bart replied, "That was me!" He explained to Pat Sajak that he, along with everyone else, was captivated with me in 1976. I was doing tricks that boys couldn't even do, and there was a lot of admiration for my athleticism. The whole world, Bart recalled, thought "isn't Nadia pre-cious?" I remember thinking that I'd traveled too far from the place Bart recalled. I did not feel precious in the slightest.

At the end of the Sajak show, Bart gave me his tele-phone number. He had a place in Venice Beach and told me he'd be around all weekend if I wanted to grab some coffee or get lunch. I was shy and suspicious of him, but

I also sensed that he was being open and honest. For a second, I was tempted to ask for help . . . I needed to move on and find a better life for myself. Bart told me later that he tried to call me after the show, but Constantin never let me know of his calls.

Meanwhile, a Romanian friend named Alexandru and his wife (they had lived in Canada for many years) invited me to Montreal to revisit my memories of the 1976 Olympics. Constantin and I decided to make the trip. We stayed with a friend of Alexandru's who owned a large home in the city. When he finally had an opportunity to get me alone, Alexandru asked what was next for me. I told him that I was thinking about staying in Montreal but hadn't yet mentioned the idea to Constantin because he'd already booked us on a flight back to Los Angeles. The next day, Alexandru sent me to meet with the director of the Olympic stadium, who told me that I could do some exhibitions and appearances for him. It wouldn't be much money, but it would be a start.

I understand your curiosity, my friend, and wish I knew exactly what happened next. All I know is that when I woke up the next morning and went downstairs, Alexandru told me that Constantin was gone. I never heard from him again, but I hope he is well and thank him for his help. I realize that our business relationship may have tarnished my name and image, but I safely escaped from Romania, and that is truly what was most important. There wasn't too much time to try to figure out why Constantin had left because very soon after his departure, CNN contacted me, and I was overwhelmed by excitement. A reporter at the network had heard about the forced separation from my family and figured out a way to allow me a two-minute conversation with my mother and brother! After months, I would finally be able to tell them that I was safe and to make sure that they were, too.

Unfortunately, the opportunity to talk to me actually began as an incredibly frightening experience for my family. Someone who didn't speak Romanian tracked them down and told them that they were going to be given a chance to speak with me. My mother thought that the CNN people were from the secret police (the Securitate had not been completely wiped out in Romania at the time). Since she didn't speak English and my brother had only a passing knowledge of the language, they didn't know what CNN was, and unfortunately, the correspondents couldn't explain.

Believing they had no choice, my mother and brother went along with the men to a hotel room. They were given snacks and champagne. My mother was certain that they were going to be killed and that this was to be their last meal before death. When she and my brother were taken to the roof of the hotel, they felt certain they were going to be pushed over the edge. But the CNN crews just needed to broadcast where signals could reach their satellite.

When I got on the phone, I could see my family but they couldn't see me. My mother was shaking, and when she heard my voice, she cried that she'd thought I was dead because the police had told her they'd shot me. "I'm not dead, I'm fine. I can't wait to see you!" I cried. The connection was too brief to go into details. The revolution that erupted in Romania in 1989 had left the country in chaos, and I didn't know when I'd actually get to see my family again. But at least they knew I was alive, and I knew that they were safe.

Alexandru and his wife invited me to move into their home. They had two little apartments, one on the bottom of the house for them and another on the top for Alexandru's mother. They moved his mother into their apartment and gave me my own place. I was awed by their generosity. They did not have a lot of money, but Alexandru gave me a credit card and told me that I should use it to buy food and new clothes. His wife and I became close friends, and she made me feel like I had finally come home.

Instead of dreaming about the United States, I began to dream of Canada. I lived with people who liked me and who didn't want anything from me. I made a few friends at the corner grocery store because I bought many lottery tickets there: If I didn't play, I couldn't win, after all. I spoke the French I had learned in school and could communicate with everyone. I even met Celine Dion, who was a big star in Canada at the time. She introduced me to the audience at her show as one of her heroes when she was eight years old. As I stood on stage with her, I thought to myself that if I worked really hard, I just might get to be a somebody in my new homeland.

At the time, life was so good, but frankly, I couldn't sit with my butt in two chairs. I couldn't keep my refugee status in America and live in Canada. The United States had granted me political asylum, and I felt I owed it a lot for that, but the idea of moving yet again to a place where I knew no one was too daunting. My biggest goal was to earn some income so that I could take care of my family, and I thought I could do that best in Montreal. So, I gave up my refugee status and became a resident of Canada. It would only have been a matter of time anyway before my political asylum status was revoked. After the 1989 revolution, Romania was no longer a Communist country, so theoretically, I had nothing to flee from anymore.

I wasn't sure how to take the next step to find a career. Alexandru was a fitness instructor, and he suggested that I think about doing some kind of traveling gymnastics show. No way, I said, my gymnastics career is over. How about we just start by working out? he encouraged. Believe it or not, it had been six years since I'd done anything athletic. I agreed to begin exercising and riding a bicycle but not to do gymnastics. All my life, gymnastics had been about achieving at least a perceived level of perfection. If I wasn't an elite gymnast, then why do gymnastics? I didn't understand that I could find joy in my sport without being the best in the world. Life had always been very black or white for me in Romania, and I needed to learn that there was a world of experiences in the gray areas that could be just as fulfilling.

In the spring of 1990, Bart Conner went to Montreal because ABC was interested in doing an in-depth piece about me. The network had years of footage of me as a gymnast and now wanted the whole story. The people at ABC also wanted Bart to help do research and conduct the interview with me. If possible, they suggested he try to get me to put together an exhibition performance. Friend, it's impossible to tell you Bart's exact impressions of me at the time. But since I have a little bit of influence over him (marriage will do that), I asked him to describe out first "in-depth" conversation and his thoughts at the time:

> *I went to Montreal to interview Nadia and got the opportunity to spend a lot of time with her. . . . That's*

when I started thinking there's a really fascinating person behind all this. She was very uncomfortable at showing too much to people. I'm the kind of guy, I have like a thousand friends, and she only wants three. I found Nadia totally captivating. It's very interesting because we were so different and still are. But I found her to be very mysterious and interesting based on the fact that I had this tremendous admiration for what she did, and I know how hard it is to do what she did because I was a pretty good gymnast but I didn't revolutionize my sport. I won some medals because I worked hard, but I can't imagine the level Nadia attained.

At the time, all of Nadia's gymnastics friends and acquaintances hoped that she was okay and wanted to do anything for her because she was such a symbol of our sport. It hurt us personally that one of us, a member of true gymnastic royalty, might not be okay. I did a long, in-depth interview with Nadia that ran on ABC, and we kept communicating after I left Montreal. Just phone calls here and there. I sensed that Nadia was looking for support, and I was more than happy to provide it. Only later did I realize that she was counting on my friendship.

You are right, friend, I found Bart "captivating," too. But nothing romantic occurred between us at the time. I remember that during one of our telephone conversations, he asked me if I'd be interested in doing some exhibition tours with him. I told Bart that my gymnastics career was over. "If I'm not going to bring home medals," I explained, "I might as well get an office job." Bart tried to convince me that gymnastics could be about more than medals, glory, and perfection. Just come to Oklahoma and train with me, he suggested. He promised it would be fun. And it was. It felt good to get my body back into shape. I didn't try to perform the routines I'd done when I was eighteen years old. There's no way I could have regained the strength and conditioning I had back then, and at age twenty-eight, there was no way I wanted to try. Competitive gymnastics is for the young. But I learned that enjoying recreational gymnastics could be for everyone. Bart and I started to bond. Still, I had no plans to leave Montreal. Alexandru and his wife were my new family, and I felt safe and comfortable with them. But my feelings for Bart were growing, too.

My twenty-ninth birthday in Montreal later that year was the best of my life. Alexandru held an enormous party with 200 people for me at the Olympic stadium. He had a friend who composed a song for me, my very own song. He also surprised me by inviting Bart. I liked Bart, but I didn't know if he felt anything other than friendship for me. He likes everybody and is nice to everyone, so it was hard to tell. When he left after the party, he told Alexandru that he "surrendered." I didn't know what that meant. Alexandru explained that it meant he was giving up trying to fight his attraction to me. He wanted to pursue some kind of a relationship. I said, "That's great, then he should call me more often."

Bart started to call me every week. Our friendship began to blossom, but things happened very slowly. Perhaps that's because we both knew that if we were to have a relationship, it would be serious. During that year, we basically fell in love with each other over the phone. We didn't know exactly where we were going, but we knew we were getting closer and closer. We did a short gymnastics exhibition called "The Mystery and Magic of Nadia" in Reno, Nevada. We performed routines to music together and grew closer as a result of that tour. Our relationship wasn't based on the physical because we weren't together that much but instead was founded on friendship and trust. But tragedy interrupted our courtship.

In Montreal, I used to go fishing every Sunday with Alexandru's family—his wife and his son from a previous relationship. I love fishing because it's so peaceful and reminds me of my childhood in Romania. In Canada, we'd play some music, have a little barbecue, and spend the entire day by the river. Alexandru was a real adventurer, and he'd also go snorkeling and scuba diving while we fished. On the Saturday of Labor Day weekend in 1991, we all went fishing by the lake but chose to return that night instead of camping. Alexandru and his son decided to go back to the river again the next day. His son planned to fish, and Alexandru wanted to do some more diving by the walls of a big dam.

Later, Alexandru's son would recall of that day that one minute he could see his father and the next he was gone; no bubbles from the oxygen tank showed on the surface of the river. Alexandru usually went to the surface every ten minutes or so to let family know he was okay. After forty-five minutes, his son was panicked. Finally, he saw a man floating on the top of the water and called to his father, assuming he was still scuba diving. Alexandru didn't respond, so his son swam out to him, only to discover he was dead. There was a lot of turbulent water near the dam, and Alexandru had hit his head against a concrete pillar and drowned.

Alexandru's son called his wife and me; he was completely broken up. It's all a blur in my mind now. We screamed and yelled off the balcony of our home, we saw reporters talking about the accident on the news, we couldn't believe it had happened. It was such a terrible tragedy. I called Bart, but he was hosting the Jerry Lewis Telethon in Chicago and was unavailable. I felt as if I was being ripped apart by sorrow and could hardly bear to hear the sobbing of Alexandru's son and wife. Alexandru had been our leader, partner, best friend, and father figure. He just couldn't be gone.

Death is such a strange thing. It leaves you with a hole in your heart that you're certain will never be filled, and it won't. But is also makes you reach out to life because our time on this planet is so short and the clock moves too quickly. I tried to call Bart again and again. Finally, just after he finished doing twenty-one hours straight on television for the telethon, he answered the phone. I was sobbing when I told him Alexandru had died. "What am I going to do?" I asked. Alexandru and I had been working together on creating business opportunities, but without him, that was over, and I couldn't be a burden on his wife and son. It wasn't fair to live on their income. Bart told me to get on a plane for Oklahoma. We'd figure things out together.

Following Alexandru's funeral, I packed up my boxes and got a ticket to Oklahoma. Alexandru's wife and I said our tearful good-byes, and I thanked her for being such a good friend to me. To this day, we are still in touch. She remarried a few years after Alexandru's death and now has two small children. I think that's what Alexandru would have wanted for her. He was so full of laughter and love and would want to know that his wife is happy. He was the kind of person who would also understand that anyone who loved him will never forget him.

When I moved to Oklahoma, Paul Ziert, Bart's former gymnastics coach, personal manager, and good friend, gave me a room in his home. Bart, who had a place in Los Angeles, was also occasionally living at Paul's home, and our rooms were next to each other. But I was mourning Alexandru's death and leaving my new family in Montreal, so I was in no place to begin a serious relationship. At the time, our proximity to each other didn't matter, and new love wasn't important. What was important was that both Bart and Paul welcomed me into their lives with open arms. Paul became my manager, too, and soon was one of my dearest friends.

Bart and Paul developed opportunities together, such as gymnastics tours, and found companies that wanted spokespeople. At first, there was no work for me, but I tagged along and was included in most of Bart's work. It was like learning a new language or a floor routine to music I had never heard before. I had no clue exactly what "appearances" were back then, but I learned from watching other celebrities, from the television, and from reading magazines. I studied how people walked, talked, and dressed, and I tried to emulate them. I worked on becoming a strong public speaker. I practiced my diction, eye contact, and gestures and always watched the way Bart, who is very professional, worked. Once in a while, Paul set up personal appearances and promotional events for me with companies such as Danskin, the Step Company, and Jockey. Paul and Bart supported me and gave me a place to live. I was learning a lot and improving my English.

Bart and I didn't restart our tentative relationship for months. We lived in the same house and traveled together, but I started to think we were just going to continue as friends. You can't begin a relationship unless it's mutual. We were visiting Los Angeles, walking along the beach by his house, when he finally kissed me. I remember marveling that it all was really happening and that I was to be given a chance at that kind of happiness. We had dinner at a romantic bistro on the beach. Things were so perfect that I thought I might wake from a dream at any moment.

You asked what first attracted me to Bart. I can't say any one thing . . . it was more that nothing *didn't* attract me to him. I thought he was gorgeous, of course, but more than that, I liked the person he was, the way he treated other people, how he never panicked. Bart always has solutions for problems and wants to help people. He was probably the easiest person for me to trust after I left Romania. I don't know why, he just was. When he came to Montreal the first time, I could tell by his voice what kind of person he was; I could read it. Bart never once told me what to do with my life. About any situation, he'd say, "This is how I'd do it, but it's a free country, so do it your way."

You want to know all of the details about Bart and me, and I understand that. When I see celebrities of any sort in romantic relationships, I want to know the details, too. It's natural to be curious, but it's also natural for me to want to keep some things to myself. Suffice it to say that over the following four years, our relationship grew into a very loving one. We respect each other's differences and quirks and always allow each other the freedom to travel, take different jobs, and do what's necessary to maintain our individuality.

I won't leave you with nothing, though. Our engagement took place after we'd been together for four years.

I knew that we were headed in that direction, so I never worried, but I have to admit it was awfully nice to be asked by Bart to spend the rest of my life with him. Let me say that it is almost impossible to trick me or pull one over on me. I'm pretty clever, and not much escapes my eyes. I must say, though, that Bart really did an amazing job of fooling me. I never saw the proposal coming.

I had gone to Japan to do some promotional work. Bart and I were scheduled to be in Germany for the World Gymnastics Championships but decided we'd take a brief weekend vacation together in Amsterdam before going to the championships. Both of our schedules had been hectic, and we needed some downtime together. Bart's mother went, too, because she was going to the championships as well. After the Worlds, Bart and I planned to go to Romania together—it was going to be his first trip to my country, and he would meet my parents and brother. It would also be my first trip back, five full years after my defection.

I'll admit that it made me very nervous to even think about returning to Romania. Not because I was afraid for my life and freedom because those days were over. I was afraid because I thought the Romanian people would consider me a traitor. In the past, everyone who left had been labeled a traitor by the government. True, Romania had a new government now, but I worried about how the people would feel when they saw me again. Would they think that I had betrayed them? Such were my concerns when I was in Amsterdam because I knew that time was short, the championships would be over soon, and then I'd have to face the past. Friend, I'd been told you can never run away from the past, but until that moment, I don't think I'd ever believed that saying completely. Regardless, at the time, Bart's and my future was definitely not in the forefront of my mind.

But Bart had it all planned out. He'd contacted a jeweler in Texas and designed a gorgeous ring that he brought to Amsterdam. It was sized perfectly because while I was in Japan, he'd taken one of my rings and given it to the jeweler. We stayed in a lovely hotel and had reservations at a great restaurant for dinner. Bart was dressed early, which was not like him at all, and was waiting for me to finish blow-drying my hair. "Are you alright?" I recall asking him. Dinner wasn't until 7:00 P.M., and it was only 5:30. Bart told me he was fine. But he really wasn't because he'd arranged for our friend, Paul Ziert, to send champagne to the room, and it hadn't yet arrived. He thought something had gone wrong. As it turned out, everyone—including Bart's mother, Paul, and our agents at International Management Group—knew about Bart's plans. With that many people in the know, I can't believe someone didn't spill the beans!

I got dressed for dinner, and just before we headed out to make our reservation, there was a knock on the door. A waiter brought in a chilled bottle of champagne. I was confused. We didn't do things like that. After the waiter uncorked the bottle and left, Bart proposed. I was in total shock. People in Romania don't get engaged; they just get married. I'd never seen a diamond engagement ring up close because in my homeland, women just wore a simple band. The engagement ring Bart held out to me was breathtaking. I think I said, "Oh no, oh my God." And then, "Yes, of course I'll marry you."

Bart and I floated through dinner that night. He was still so flustered that he gave the waiter something close to a 50 percent tip. All I know is that the entire evening felt like a dream. It seemed my Prince Charming had finally kissed me and I'd awakened after a long sleep. I had lived under so much control in my own country and struggled a great deal when I defected, but all of a sudden, everything I'd been through in my entire life was culminating in total happiness. I felt as if I was in a corny movie with a happy ending, and it was hard to believe that it was *my* happy ending. Bart, of course, had a lot to do with it, but I also realized that I had controlled my destiny, too. I was the one who'd made it possible for me to be in that hotel in Amsterdam on that night to receive Bart's proposal. We create our own fairy tales.

Do you grasp, my friend, how far I'd come at that moment? A little girl born in the poor village of Onesti, Romania, to a mechanic and a homemaker went from a kid climbing trees to the number one gymnast in the world. I survived and thrived during my younger years under Ceausescu's regime, suffered through Romania's shortage of food and fuel, and tried to carve out a decent life for myself and my family in a country run by leaders who lacked any and all conscience toward their people. I risked my life to defect, running into the unknown and darkness and the real possibility of going to jail or getting a bullet in my back. I left my family behind and believed I'd never see them again. I lost my new family in Montreal when Alexandru drowned. After that, I took a risk and moved to Oklahoma, not knowing what lay ahead. And then I found another family in Bart and Paul, a career, and more than I ever could have dreamed of . . . the love of my life. My grandmother had told me that I was born lucky. I think she was right.

A Breath of Fresh Air

I have ten rules for living. They are the product of my past and present and my hopes for the future:

1. Master the basics
2. Focus on the details
3. Expect to struggle—it is not easy to succeed
4. Acknowledge your mistakes and learn from them
5. Define success in your own terms
6. Enjoy the process because preparation is everything
7. Do more than what is asked of you
8. Be original—make your own impact
9. Be willing to sacrifice—it makes success even sweeter
10. Maintain your love and passion for what you do

My return to Romania five years after my defection was private and intensely personal, and I didn't think anyone other than my family would be interested. Perhaps those who believed I'd betrayed them would give me sideways glances and dirty looks, or perhaps they'd even say something derogatory, but I hoped that most of my fellow Romanians would have moved on because they had much bigger priorities and more important concerns. Ceausescu and the Securitate were gone, and no one would surreptitiously follow me or bug my hotel room. No one, I anticipated, would demand to know my plans, schedule, or conversations. I had faded into the dusty history books, and Romanians wouldn't care much anymore about Nadia Comaneci.

I was so wrong. When Bart and I got off our plane in Bucharest, thousands of Romanians waving signs and tossing bouquets of flowers were at the airport; even the new prime minister was there. It was really something. *Incredible* is too simple a word to describe the moment I stepped out of the plane. I have never in my life felt so lucky or loved by so many people. I remembered the fears I had in 1976 when I was greeted by screaming crowds after the Montreal Olympics. I hadn't understood, then, what I'd meant to the people of Romania. How could any child conceive of that? But as an adult and a woman who'd finally returned to the country she loved, I grasped the personal significance as well as the import to the people. I had been a symbol of someone bright and young and talented and Romanian—a symbol of what Romanians believed they and their country could be if only they were given the chance.

ABC had asked to send a camera crew to accompany Bart and me because they wanted to document my first return home. I'd agreed with reservations, since I wasn't certain exactly what would greet us in Romania or that I wanted it on film! Now I am so glad that I have the memory saved forever on a videotape because the entire trip was such a whirlwind that I might have forgotten some of the magic of the moment. ABC caught everything. And after spending my young life being followed without ever quite seeing the secret police, it was a nice change to know that the network's cameras were in plain sight.

On our first night in Romania, Bart and I stayed in Bucharest and visited my mother and brother. Bart had met my mother before (she comes to visit us every year for at least a month). She definitely approved, as did my brother and sister-in-law, because it's impossible not to love Bart. We had a great night as a family. Once, I had believed I would never see my mother and brother again, let alone spend time in Romania with them and my fiancé. It was all a bit surreal.

Early the next morning, we formed a little caravan of four cars and began our drive to Onesti to see my father. Bart had never met him before and wanted to personally ask him for my hand in marriage. It took *forever* to get to Onesti. Every small town along the way—and there are tons of them—was filled with crowds waving flowers and hundreds of little girls singing Nadia songs. People were so proud to have me back home that they turned out in full force to make me feel welcome. The sentiment about my defection was simple: "Good for you," they all said. "We wish we would have had the guts or opportunity to leave, too."

In each small town, we stopped so that the mayor could make a speech and give me a pretty bouquet of flowers. Then we went to his office because it would have been impolite not to share a glass of champagne. Bart was overwhelmed at the crowds and speeches and all of the kissing. In Romania, people always double-kiss each other's cheeks. It's a bit different from the American custom of shaking hands or giving a manly slap on the back. At any rate, the four-hour trip took nine hours. Everyone wanted a minute with me, and I was so happy to give each of them what I could.

When we finally arrived in Onesti, I showed Bart around the village, and then we went to my father's apartment. My dad was nervous. The television cameras and strangers were overwhelming. He didn't know very many words in English, so when Bart asked him for my hand in marriage (in front of the rolling cameras), he said, "Thank you." He'd gotten his words confused. I joke to this day that at least he didn't know the English words for "Thank God."

Onesti held a huge celebration, and thousands of people packed into the gymnasium where I had trained with Bela and Marta Karolyi. Everyone made a speech, even my grade school teacher and the priest who had baptized me. I felt an enormous wave of gratitude for all of the people who had cared about me back then and still did five years after my defection. It seemed they had all developed a newfound respect for me after I defected, though I think to this day that many Romanians still have misconceptions about exactly what I left behind. They assume I sacrificed wealth, an enormous home, expensive cars, jewelry, and luxurious comfort. It makes me uncomfortable to correct those misconceptions about me, even today, because I still find the entire situation humiliating. I have fierce pride, and sometimes it can get in the way.

Bart and I were invited to visit the president and prime minister of Romania after our time in Onesti. We were received in their version of the White House, which is a gorgeous mansion. The president asked us if we'd considered having our wedding in Romania. I remember being really taken aback at the suggestion. Bart and I hadn't even talked about the wedding because we'd only recently gotten engaged and were just enjoying the moment. I said something about the fact that we lived Norman, Oklahoma, but Bart immediately said, "There's no better place in the world—we have to be married here. It would be a complete shock to Romanians if you weren't." And that was that.

I don't think Bart knew what he was getting into. We spoke with Adrian Nastase, then speaker of the House and now prime minister of Romania. He's an incredibly charming, brilliant man, and he asked Bart who was going to be his *nasu* (godparent). In the Orthodox Church, a couple chooses a prominent person who is willing to act as a godparent to them and their children. That person also throws the wedding. It is a big responsibility, but most weddings in Romania are very simple affairs, so the financial cost is nominal. Bart asked Adrian and his wife to act as our godparents, and they happily agreed. Adrian's wife was thrilled. She felt that the event had to be glamorous and beautiful, and she ran with the idea. So much for an inexpensive wedding!

Bart and I sat back and decided that not only would we not try to exert any control over the planning but also that we'd just enjoy every minute of the event. We were incredibly busy with our jobs, and other than choosing a wedding dress that was made for me by Yumi Katsura, a designer in Japan, I did absolutely no work for what turned out to be anything but a "simple affair." Adrian's wife chose the venue for the wedding, a beautiful old Romanian Orthodox monastery, and arranged for the reception and party at the Parliamentary Palace,

hosted by President Ion Iliescu. We invited fifteen hun-
dred guests, including Juan Antonio Samaranch (head of
the International Olympic Committee) and Arnold
Schwarzenegger. Bart had been on the board of the Special Olympics for sixteen years, and at the time, Arnold
was, too, and they'd become friends.

You may not know this, friend, but Orthodox weddings are two-day events. On the first day, you get married in the mayor's office in a civil ceremony. In the days
of communism, people were discouraged from getting
married in a church, and some of the old laws hadn't
been changed yet. So when it was time for our wedding,
Bart and I flew back to Romania and went to the court-
house in business clothes. We were married on live television by a Romanian official so that all the people of the
country could watch the event. Since the ceremony was
in Romanian, I translated for Bart. At one point, the official paused and looked expectantly at Bart. "He wants
to know if you want to marry me," I whispered. Of
course, the microphone picked up my voice, and I guess
everyone in the country had a good laugh. People
thought that was hysterical. Bart kept saying "Da,"
which means "yes" in Romanian, over and over again to
every question throughout the ceremony. We were both
happy and relieved when it was over.

When we left the government building, the square
outside was packed with thousands of people who
wanted to catch a glimpse of us. Bodyguards escorted us
back to our hotel, and then we stood on the balcony and
said a small speech to thank the people for coming to
our wedding. Bart had his speech written out phoneti-
cally and thanked everyone for accepting him and said,
"Today, I am half Romanian and half American." The

people thought he was wonderful, both because of what he said and because he struggled through the speech but kept on trying until he'd finished.

It may be hard for you to understand why it mattered so much to my country that I was married with all the style and class that could be afforded. The people wanted to show the world the elegance and glamour of what Romania once was and could be again in the future. Over the course of thirty years, the people and culture had been virtually destroyed, and my wedding was a chance for everyone to fall in love with Romania again: I am not the only one with fierce pride in my country. I want to make it clear to you that though I left Romania, I never left the people and my roots—I left the system. I have always loved my country, and that's why, to this day, I haven't given up my citizenship. I am Romanian first and foremost, and Romania was where my wedding was meant to be. I knew that I could take my immediate family to a wedding in the United States, but I could not take the entire country. I needed to go to them.

My formal wedding the day after the official one was the stuff of any little girl's dreams. In addition to our Romanian guests, Bart and I invited eighty friends from America. All of us stayed at a hotel for one week; in fact, it was renamed "Hotel Nadia" from "Hotel Lido" because we took over the entire place. The day of the wedding, I wore a gorgeous gown with a 23-foot train covered with 10,000 pearls, carried by little Romanian gymnasts. Yumi Katsura, the designer, even sent someone to help me put the dress on because it was so complicated that I literally couldn't have dressed myself!

There were 10,000 people in the plaza outside the hotel waiting to see me before I left for the church. We couldn't take any formal pictures before the wedding because once I stepped into the plaza, people were very excited to see me and it became too hard to set things up. As a result, all of the photographs from our wedding are snapshots from friends or the footage from ABC, which filmed the whole event. Half of the city of Bucharest was closed—stores, streets, everything. The procession to the wedding felt like something that would happen in England with princes and princesses. It was truly magical and filled with pomp and circumstance.

The actual wedding was gorgeous. Adrian's wife had filled the monastery with flowers and music. Once again, Bart did his best to follow along with the Orthodox traditions, but this time, things were much more complicated than they'd been at the civil wedding, when he'd just needed to stand in one place and say "yes." Everything in the church is done three times—for example, walking around the altar during the service. There's also a lot of kissing of the priest's hand, and the bride and groom wear crowns. It can be very confusing even if you're familiar with the religion. People advise brides and grooms that the one who remembers a particular tradition first should step on the other person's foot to warn or remind them. The bride or groom who does the bulk of the stepping, it is said, will be the one most in control of the marriage. I did all of the stepping on Bart's foot. Unfortunately, I forgot to tell him about our "signal," so the first time during the wedding that I stepped on his toes, he asked, "What was that for?" I told him I was going to stomp on his foot before we were supposed to do anything three times. He whispered that I could have told him before the ceremony. "It's too late," I whispered back with a smile, "I'm going to tower over this marriage."

The reception line after the wedding was one of the funnier parts of the day. There was Bart, an American kid from Chicago who was now living in Oklahoma, and he had to greet strange men who all wanted to kiss his cheeks. There was a gigantic lineup, and Bart just put on a smile and let everyone exfoliate his smooth cheeks with their beards. By the time his American friends got to him (these guys had never even hugged each other before), Bart grabbed each one and planted kisses on *their* cheeks! It was incredible to see him display so much affection, and to this day, they're all closer for the time they spent in Romania. To be introduced to such strong, passionate people really changed their lives.

My friend, I wish I could transport you to our reception so that you could live it for yourself. The food and wines were delicious, and the music ranged from ballroom pieces and opera to traditional folk songs. There were dancers, singers, and actors from all over Europe in addition to the group of friends we'd brought from America. Bart and I tasted all of the food, danced, and flitted from table to table talking with our guests. I have never smiled so much in my life—quite a contrast to the person who, as a child, was known for not smiling. I have heard that for your wedding, all of the stars align to make the day perfect. Though I still don't believe in perfection, that day was as close as I think I'll ever come to experiencing it.

In the middle of the night, while everyone was drinking, dancing, and laughing, something wonderful and strange and unexpected happened. I was stolen away from my groom by a group of men. I am not pulling your leg. It is a Romanian tradition that if the groom loses sight of his bride on the night of their wedding reception, she may be stolen. The men (old and dear friends of mine) put me in a boat, and we motored out into the middle of a lake, where a yacht was waiting. Meanwhile, Bart was dancing with his mother when a security guard tapped him on the shoulder and asked, "Do you know where your wife is?"

Bart looked around and couldn't see me. "I don't know," he replied. "Where is she?"

"She's been stolen," the guard told him. "You should pay more attention to your bride, otherwise she'll disappear." The guard handed Bart a cell phone, and the man on the line joked, "If you want Nadia back, you'll have to pay a ransom." Bart offered $1,000. "That's not enough," the man exclaimed, "she's worth more than that!"

"How about $10,000 donated to the charity of your choice?" Bart asked.

"It's a deal."

The men motored me back to the dock, where Bart stood waiting. He gathered me in his arms and promised never to lose sight of me again. The party continued until five in the morning. Sometimes I'd stop dancing and look around, trying to take it all in and remember everything. It was hard to comprehend that all of it was for me and for Bart, that people were so generous with their time and feelings. There had been moments when I thought I was so jaded that nothing could ever surprise or delight me again. I am so fortunate that I was wrong.

I feel as if I've lived the joy of a thousand lives. The difficulties seem like moments that barely touch the hours, days, and years of good times. I never forget that I need to share my good fortune with others. I'm involved in many charities, such as the Special Olympics, and I host the Jerry Lewis Telethon for the Muscular Dystrophy

Association every year. I'm really proud to be a part of the Laureus World Sports Academy, where elite athletes raise money for great causes all over the world. I also do fund-raising for AIDS-related organizations, especially those involving children. In addition, I help Bart run the Bart Conner Gymnastics Academy in Norman, Oklahoma, and together, we help gymnasts get college athletic scholarships that, in my mind, are so much more valuable for most children than shooting for a handful of Olympic spots and medals.

I could list all of the additional charities I help and the other work I do, but that would take away from the reason I do it all in the first place. It's not for acclaim or for medals; it's because I want to give back. I've discovered that doing for others is much more fulfilling than standing alone on a podium while crowds cheer your individual accomplishments. I'm part of a bigger plan now, and joining hands with people from around the globe who understand that giving and sharing can change the world is exactly where I choose to be.

Friend, you started writing to me because you wanted to know how I came to be Nadia Comaneci. You wanted to find out the secrets that made me tick; understand all of my experiences; figure out the effects of Romania, communism, Ceausescu's rule, defection, and love upon my life. Do you know more about me now than when we began? I think I do . . . but I am a mysterious and complex human being, and like everyone else, I constantly evolve. I've always achieved more in life than I had in mind. But I know that I can be more, do a better job, and contribute a greater amount to society.

I thank you for your letters and for wanting to know about me because as a result of looking back, I have cleaned house; I have cleared away the cobwebs and old cardboard boxes holding tattered pictures, medals, broken dreams, disappointments, fears, past glories, and childhood wishes. There's more room to breathe now and to open some windows and locked doors and let a clean breeze sweep through closed up spaces. And now there's fresh air and light.

About the Author

At the 1976 Olympics in Montreal, Canada, a fourteen-year-old Romanian dynamo captured the hearts and minds of the world with her daring and perfection. We came to know her simply as "Nadia."

By the time the 1976 Olympics ended, Comaneci had earned seven perfect 10s, three gold medals, one bronze, one silver, and countless fans. She appeared on the covers of *Time*, *Newsweek*, and *Sports Illustrated*, all in the same week, and returned home to Romania to a heroine's welcome.

Four years later, at the 1980 Moscow Olympics, Comaneci earned two more gold medals and two silver to bring her Olympic total to nine medals (five gold, three silver, one bronze). In 1996, she was inducted into the International Gymnastics Hall of Fame.

In April of that same year, Comaneci married American gymnast Bart Conner, himself an Olympic champion, in a Romanian state wedding. Comaneci now divides her time among appearances, commercial endorsements for major companies, speaking engagements, and charity events.

Currently, Nadia and Bart are partners with their manager, Paul Ziert, in the Bart Conner Gymnastics Academy, *International Gymnast* magazine, Perfect 10 Productions, Inc. (a TV production company), and Grips, Etc. (a gymnastics manufacturing company).

In 1999, Comaneci was honored by ABC News and *Ladies Home Journal* as one of the "100 Most Important Women of the 20th Century." Comaneci, who is also fluent in French and English, continues to travel the world pursuing her various interests. Her charity work includes her positions as vice chair of the Board of Directors of Special Olympics International, vice president of the Muscular Dystrophy Association, and board member of the Laureus Sports for Good Foundation.

She and Bart live in Norman, Oklahoma.